THE BITCH
IN YOUR HEAD

Also by Dr. Jacqueline Hornor Plumez

Mother Power
Divorcing a Corporation
Successful Adoption

THE BITCH IN YOUR HEAD

How to Finally Squash Your Inner Critic

DR. JACQUELINE HORNOR PLUMEZ

TAYLOR TRADE PUBLISHING
Lanham • Boulder • New York • London

Many people shared their stories with me. Some of their names and identifying information have been changed to protect the privacy of those who wished to remain anonymous.

Published by Taylor Trade Publishing
An imprint of The Rowman & Littlefield Publishing Group, Inc.
4501 Forbes Boulevard, Suite 200, Lanham, Maryland 20706
www.rowman.com

Unit A, Whitacre Mews, 26-34 Stannary Street, London SE11 4AB, United Kingdom

Distributed by NATIONAL BOOK NETWORK

British Library Cataloguing in Publication Information Available

Library of Congress Cataloging-in-Publication Data
Plumez, Jacqueline Hornor.
    The bitch in your head : how to finally squash your inner critic / Dr. Jacqueline Hornor Plumez.
      pages cm
    Includes bibliographical references.
    ISBN 978-1-4930-0790-5 (pbk. : alk. paper) — ISBN 978-1-63076-119-6 (electronic)
    1. Criticism, Personal. 2. Self-talk. 3. Negativism. 4. Women—Psychology. 5. Self-esteem in women. I. Title.
    BF637.C74P58 2015
    158.1—dc23

                                                                    2014046663

♾TM The paper used in this publication meets the minimum requirements of American National Standard for Information Sciences—Permanence of Paper for Printed Library Materials, ANSI/NISO Z39.48-1992.

Printed in the United States of America

With thanks and love to my daughter, Nicole

CONTENTS

1

INTRODUCING THE BITCH

You look fat.
How could you be so stupid?
You really blew it!
No one wants to hear what you have to say.
Don't even try—it'll never work.

You've probably said bitchy things like this to yourself. But would you ever undercut a friend that way? No. It would be too hurtful. So why would you do it to yourself?

Some people hear The Bitch in their head and think she's motivating—encouraging them to work harder or smarter. Other people think she protects them from being disappointed or arrogant. But most people are so used to self-criticism that they hardly hear The Bitch and have no idea how discouraging, demoralizing, and self-destructive she can be.

The Bitch can make life miserable in many ways. She can keep you from having a good day or a good night's sleep, from getting the love you want or the raise you deserve. By focusing on the negative and frightening, The Bitch prevents you from seeing what is positive and possible about yourself, your life, and your future.

Everyone—even people who seem utterly secure and accomplished—has a Bitch in her head, preying on her secret vulnerabilities. For some people, she appears in only one or two areas of their lives, but you can bet those are important areas. Other people have such a pervasive Bitch, they can hardly function.

But The Bitch can be banished! For years, I've helped patients do just that. Once they start encouraging rather than criticizing themselves, their careers, social lives, and love lives almost magically improve. As one patient told me, "I didn't realize I was carrying around an emotional backpack full of rocks, weighing me down. Now everything feels so much easier and lighter."

Yes. It's so much easier to run the race of life without all that heavy Bitch-baggage weighing you down, battering your self-esteem and sapping your energy.

TWO PATIENTS WHO INTRODUCED ME TO THE BITCH

Jennifer was an attractive, twenty-eight-year-old lawyer who came to me because she felt depressed. With gray eyes looking earnestly through black-rimmed glasses, she said, "I don't think I'm depressed enough for medication, and even if I am, I don't want to take it. But I'm always feeling kind of down and I don't have the energy I used to."

Jennifer described how she worked long hours, putting constant pressure on herself to succeed and harshly criticizing any mistake she made. She rarely had time on weeknights for fun and friends, much less love. And by the time the weekend rolled around, even if she didn't have to work, she was so exhausted that, while she might go out one night, she usually just stayed home and watched TV. Sometimes she only left her apartment to go to the gym.

When I asked if she ever gave herself time off for fun, she said, "Mostly I just keep up with friends on Facebook." I empathized and understood why she felt depressed.

The other patient, Lana, suffered from low self-esteem. The first time I saw her in my waiting room, my brain registered, "Las Vegas show girl." But like many beautiful women, this curvy blonde was insecure about her looks. She rarely left her house without makeup and said she would "never, ever go to a department store without being very well dressed."

Lana's husband had left her for another woman, and Lana was sure any new man would reject her if he discovered the truth: She was flat chested. Her hips were balanced by a well-padded bra. She was saving up for breast-implant surgery and didn't want to date until that operation.

Psychologists say things such as "It's not healthy to be so hard on yourself" to patients like Jennifer. To Lana they might say, "Why do you think that's true?" or "When did you start having such a negative self-image?" I've tried these gentle approaches. They usually don't work.

Then one Friday morning, after a week when every other patient I'd seen had been self-critical, I noticed that Jennifer and Lana were next on my schedule.

I was planning to talk to Jennifer, once again, about her "tyranny of the shoulds"—how her life was controlled by what she thought she *should* do instead of what she *wanted* to do. And about how she was afraid that her life would unravel if she lightened up on herself even a little bit. But when our session began a few minutes after eight, Jennifer started berating herself in a new way.

> "I'm an idiot," she claimed. "I should have gotten an MBA instead of going to law school. I'd be making a lot more money."
>
> "I thought you liked what you do," I said.
>
> "I do . . ."
>
> "And didn't you tell me you hated economics in college?"
>
> "Yes . . ."
>
> Instead of exploring why she was always so mean to herself, I blurted out, "Boy, are you a bitch!"

Jennifer's eyes widened. Her body pulled back into her chair as if I had struck her. I waited a few seconds before adding, "to yourself." We had one of our most productive sessions after that. For the first time, she seemed to understand how inappropriately hard she was on herself.

During my next session, Lana, who had the day off but still showed up in full makeup and a beautifully tailored suit, said she'd turned down a date with a cute guy at her gym. My "Bitch" line had worked so well with Jennifer that I decided to use it again. Lana initially reacted in horror that her psychologist, the previously kind Dr. Plumez, was cursing at her. But then, as with Jennifer, the shock value helped break through her resistance so the process of self-acceptance could begin.

"Would you ever tell your daughter that she was too unattractive to appear in public without makeup? Or that she shouldn't even bother trying to date without a D-cup?" I asked.

"No."

"Why?"

"It would make her feel bad . . . discourage her," Lana replied.

"And how do you think she would feel if you followed her around all day, saying the mean things to her that you say to yourself?"

"She'd probably be so depressed she couldn't get out of bed."

"Right!"

Finally, by labeling and personifying what Lana and Jennifer were doing to themselves—by calling it The Bitch—they could begin to hear what was going on in their heads. Naming and "externalizing" a problem makes it easier to recognize and fight. And hearing and recognizing The Bitch is the first and most important step to banishing her.

SHE'S EVERYWHERE!

When I began to tell friends about my concept of *The Bitch in Your Head*, I wondered if they would look at me as if I were crazy. (My Bitch was saying this concept was no big deal.) But every woman I spoke to began nodding her head in agreement and understood exactly what I was talking about. Most started telling me stories about how their Bitch tortured them. The next time I saw them they would often say that recognizing her—and laughing at her—diminished her power.

When I began to receive this same reaction from people I didn't know, I knew I was on to something. For example, when I began chatting with the mayor of a small town at a reception, she asked me what I did. Instead of making polite conversation, I said, "I'm writing a book called *The Bitch in Your Head*. It's about how women beat themselves up."

Her eyes widened. I assumed the title of my book had offended her, until she said, "I can't even get out of bed in the morning before it starts. I open my eyes and immediately think of all the mistakes I made the day before."

Likewise, I met a woman at a conference who has had a long career in consulting, traveling worldwide on projects for hospitals, universities, and a major foundation. I told her I was doing research for my book and asked her about The Bitches she has seen in businesswomen. Instead of telling me about other people, she said, "Every time I get a consulting job, my Bitch says, 'Can you really do this? Who do you think you are?' And I have to say to her, 'Yes. I think I *can* do this. At least I'm going to try.'"

As I collected Bitch stories, some of the men I talked to didn't seem to know what I was talking about. But only one woman—literally, just one out of the hundreds I talked to—didn't even nod or smile in recognition. Maybe she was the most secure person I ever met. Or maybe her Bitch was telling her to keep her mouth shut!

RECOGNIZING THIS AS A SYNDROME

After talking to many people, I understood that while people criticize and discourage themselves in many different ways and in many different situations, they all have something in common: they wrestle with the same syndrome.

The Bitch is behind recriminations like, "I should have moved to Los Angeles" or "I never should have stopped dating Will." She causes people to get stuck in self-blame, sapping the energy they need to analyze and correct their mistakes. And when people "catastrophize" (He will *kill* me! . . . The party is going to be a *complete* failure . . . I've made the *biggest* mistake of my life), by exaggerating problems, The Bitch makes people too afraid to take steps to counteract them.

The Bitch also causes phobias, making people deathly afraid of everything from airplanes to zoos. Traditionally, the fear of death and public speaking have been the most common phobias, and I'll talk in later chapters about those. But now it seems that many Americans have a greater fear: going to a party if they don't know anyone there. The Party Bitch is so powerful that many people would literally rather die than walk into a party alone.

The more I listened, the more I heard how The Bitch is everywhere, making people's lives miserable. She has endless variations, tormenting young and old, rich and poor, criticizing every aspect of love, life, and work. But she's particularly awful to women when they look in a mirror.

Let's imagine a large mirror. A man with bowed legs and a giant beer belly hanging over his plaid boxer shorts is looking into it. What do you think he sees? Believe it or not, Dr. Rita Freedman, a nationally known expert in body image, told me that most men would ignore the legs and belly and focus on what they like about their appearance. They will pop an arm muscle and admire it. Or they will stare at their blue eyes and think, "I'm looking hot!"

Now imagine an attractive woman looking in the mirror. What do you think she is focusing on? Only what she doesn't like. She will zoom in on a little cellulite on her thighs and tell herself that she looks fat. Or she will examine the lines beginning to form around her mouth and eyes. Odds are she won't smile and call them laugh lines. Oh, no; she'll call them ugly wrinkles or crow's feet. And speaking of pejorative terms . . .

WHY DO I USE THE TERRIBLE WORD *BITCH*?

I hate that word, too. It's sexist and ugly. But I use it because it gets the desired result. As I said before, when patients rattled on, spouting self-criticism, I used to say milder, more conventional things like, "You are being too self-critical." Sometimes they nodded in agreement but dismissed my comments because they thought I was just being nice.

Others, who had critical parents, dismissed my feedback, thinking that their negative thoughts were deserved or protective. Simply exploring the childhood origins of their Bitch didn't help much, either. Patients might understand where their self-criticism came from, but that didn't stop the problem.

But when I started using the psychological technique of personifying the problem—giving their problem a name (The Bitch) and identifying their self-destructive thoughts as a mean person—they got it. (When you read the title of this book, didn't you get it, too?) Suddenly they began to hear how self-defeating they were being. And only when a person truly understands how destructive The Bitch is does she become ready to apply the psychological tools and techniques I prescribe to banish this problem.

If you find a better word than *Bitch*, let me know. Believe me, I've searched for one, especially with male clients. But what is the masculine equivalent? After lengthy discussions with men, nothing seems to have the same bite. Bastard? Asshole? Undercutter? Criticizer? They just don't have the right connotation—or punch—needed for self-recognition.

And self-recognition is the key. Here's an example that a friend, who sings in a choir, sent me via e-mail: "Ever since you told me about your book, I have been keeping track of how often my inner Bitch is speaking. Wow. It is amazing how I got used to having that voice obsessively running in my head: *Why didn't you . . . ? How could you say . . . ?* It is constantly running on like a broken record. What is really amazing is that it happens even with minor things that *make no difference!* I can brood about something for days because I wasn't perfect."

Her e-mail continued, "For example, I recently came back from a vocal performance workshop where participants were asked to pick a song and perform it in front of the group for practice in public singing. I am a somewhat nervous performer, but as it turned out I had much more experience than most of the other participants. Nonetheless, I was not satisfied with what I did.

"For three days I obsessively went over my performance in my mind, thinking *Why didn't I pick another song? Why didn't I sing such and such?*

"Then I remembered what you told me about The Bitch! I said, 'What difference did that song make? NONE! Just because those few minutes on stage weren't perfect, I'm not going to let my Bitch drag me down.' So I said, 'Hey—you went there to try something new and you had fun and learned something about yourself.'

"I can now hear how The Bitch is constantly nipping at my heels—nip, nip, nip. But I'm going to try to stop it."

IS THIS A WOMAN'S PROBLEM?

Of course not. The Bitch whispers in men's ears that their penis is too small, or everyone is staring at their bald spot, or how other men make more money. But society makes girls and women more vulnerable to self-criticism.

·   Girls are still expected to nurture and help more than boys, so they are more prone to guilt if relationships don't go well. And girls are more likely to be scolded if they "brag." As a woman remembered, "My grandmother and aunt and some teachers told me it was unbecoming to boast when I was merely stating that I thought I was good at something. No one ever told the boys that their proud attributes were something they should underplay."

When girls become women, society reinforces these pressures in many ways. For example, which parent are schools more likely to call at the office if a child is sick? And who gets more blame if a child acts badly? If you answered "the father," you get extra credit for equality. But you probably grew up on Mars. Things still aren't fair here on earth, where mothers tend to take on more of the childcare responsibilities and suffer from more guilt about juggling a career and family.

You may have read about another kind of double standard that harms women when they encounter failure. Let's say a marketing executive fails to meet the goals set by the boss. If the executive is a woman, research says she will tend to blame herself, whereas a male executive is likely to say the goal or the boss was unfair or impossible.

Flip it around and say the executive did very well and exceeded the goal. A woman will tend to say, "I was lucky," while a man will usually pat himself on the back. I learned about this double whammy—all the blame but none of the credit—in graduate school. Current books about women in business, such as Sheryl Sandberg's best-selling *Lean In* and *The Confidence Code* by reporters Katty Kay and Claire Shipman, reveal that the double whammy is still making it harder for women to be self-confident and take on high-risk/high-reward assignments.

Susan Leader, a financial services executive, summed up what she has observed at work: "When there is a difference of opinion, more often than not, men assume they are right . . . and, more often than not, women are prone to assume they are wrong." At least it seems that more women than men are prone to question whether they are the ones who made the mistake.

I was quite naïve about the psychological differences between men and women when I began my Ph.D. program. I wanted to believe that we were all equal and the same. But over the years, as I studied, spoke with colleagues, worked with almost as many male as female patients, had a long marriage, and raised both a boy and a girl, I have had many opportunities to learn that there are profound differences that give The Bitch opportunities to create hurt and misunderstanding. So, even though this is a book that is primarily about how women experience The Bitch, I will at least mention some of the Bitch sex differences in each chapter.

QUESTIONNAIRE

The Bitch occurs in many forms. She might plague you in just one way or be a Hydra with many heads, provoking constant battle. As you read through the book, you will get to know your Bitch better as you see how she affects many aspects of life. And as I mentioned, identifying your Bitch is the first step to getting rid of her.

So here's a questionnaire to get you started. Take the time to give this section serious thought. Don't be discouraged even if you discover that you do every self-destructive behavior listed. The rest of the book prescribes psychological tools and techniques to control each kind of Bitch. So for now, get out some paper and shut her up while you note what you have to change:

1. **Insulting Yourself**: The Bitch makes people call themselves terrible names: Fat Ass, Crooked Nose, Idiot. I have a friend who calls herself stupid when she makes a mistake playing bridge or muffs a tennis serve. Does she really think this is going to make her a better player? If so, why would she never call her friends or her daughter stupid for doing the same things?

   What insults do I have to stop giving myself?

   What situations require me to practice more self-compassion?

2. **Ignoring Compliments and Not Taking Credit for Accomplishments**: Self-esteem is built by absorbing compliments from others and giving them to yourself. Saying nice things to yourself is not being narcissistic. It's simply doing to yourself as you should be doing to others. Women have to take credit

for their successes instead of saying things like, "Oh, I was just lucky."

What compliments do I need to accept and absorb?

What should I give myself credit for being/doing?

3. **Lacking Assertion**: Assertive women don't allow other people to treat them like doormats, take advantage or insult them. They also don't engage in the other extreme, acting overly aggressive and insulting. Assertive people can state opinions, ask for what they want, agree or disagree, and pleasantly but firmly say "no" if someone asks them for something. They can be strong without being rude.

When do I need to be less passive?

What do I need to be less insulting or overly aggressive about?

4. **Negative Comparisons**: The Bitch makes you feel bad by saying, "Why aren't you as thin, pretty, popular, successful, blah, blah, blah as she is?" There is a big difference between making negative comparisons that demoralize you and finding positive role models who inspire you, teaching you how to behave and achieve.

I need to stop criticizing myself because I am not like these people.

Who would be a great positive role model?

5. **Perfectionism**: No matter what The Bitch says, no person or situation is ever perfect. Everyone makes mistakes. So spend your energy correcting and learning from them. Also, no one always wins. So ignore anyone who says "Second place is just the first loser" and simply try to be your personal best.

How should I lighten up on myself?

Who are the people I should ignore when they pressure me to be perfect?

6. **Pessimism**: Optimists know they are optimistic. Pessimists think they are realists. Pessimists also think they are being self-protective, but their negative thoughts are discouraging and self-defeating, because people who try and fail feel better about themselves than people who never try at all.

What do I have to stop assuming is impossible?

Memo to self: If I try and fail, I will praise myself for being brave enough to try.

7. **Questioning Where There Is No Answer**: Why did I get sick? Why did my father love my sister more than me? Why did my boyfriend leave me? Sometimes bad things happen to good people. Life isn't fair, and we might never know why. Instead of getting stuck questioning the negative past, use your energy to create a positive future.

   What things must I stop questioning?

   What people and things must I simply accept as they are?

8. **Recriminations and Unfilled Aspirations**: If you plague yourself with "I would have . . . could have . . . should have . . ." you know The Bitch is talking to you. Change the sentence to "I will . . . I want to . . . I can . . ." and make plans to achieve those goals. Or just forget it and accept that the woulda, coulda, shoulda train has left the station and isn't coming back. Plan a positive future, instead of wallowing in the past.

   What things do I want to try to get or do?

   What part of my past do I need to put behind me and focus on the future instead?

9. **Shame and Self-Blame**: The Bitch makes people become ashamed and defensive instead of taking responsibility in a healthy manner, apologizing, and making amends. Lives, careers, and relationships can be rebuilt if positive action is taken instead of writhing in unhealthy shame and self-blame.

   What things do I need to stop blaming myself for?

   What things do I need to apologize or make amends for?

10. **Insulting Others**: If you grew up in a family where people insulted each other and called each other names, you may think it is okay to do that to your mate or your child. But name-calling makes people dislike you, feel bad about themselves, and think YOU are a Bitch. It's not your fault that you were raised this way. But it *is* your fault if you don't stop. In a healthy relationship, people will accept your apology if they think you are truly sorry and want to stop. People who are Bitchy and self-critical to others tend to be that way to themselves.

    Who are the people I have to stop insulting?

    What situation brings out The Bitch in me?

Whew! Even if you need to work on almost everything, don't feel overwhelmed. You have completed the most important step in changing your life for the better: identifying your Bitch and having a clear view of what you are up against. Now you are ready for the good part: changing for the better.

HOW TO GET THE MOST OUT OF THIS BOOK

As you read on, listen to what you are saying to yourself. If you are saying something that you wouldn't say to a friend or your child (unless you identified with #10 above), you've caught your Bitch.

For example, if a friend confided that she thought she had a medical problem, you would never just minimize it and say, "Oh, don't worry about that!" or scare her to death with "Oh, my God, you're going to die!" You would encourage her to seek proper medical treatment and might even offer to go with her to the doctor.

If your daughter complained that she had gained too much weight and you agreed with her, you wouldn't say, "Yes, you look really fat and ugly!" As you will learn in Chapter 3, she would probably gain even more weight if you criticized her like that. Instead, you would help her find a healthy exercise and eating plan and stick to it with her.

Each of the following chapters presents a different area of life sabotaged by Bitchy thinking and offers tools and techniques for getting The Bitch out of your head. I strongly recommend reading all the chapters, even if you don't think your Bitch attacks you that way. You may find insight, tools, and techniques you can use in different situations.

Every one of us needs to learn how to be our own best friend, supportive coach, and loving parent. By the end of this book, you will know how to do that!

2

LITTLE BITCH

It Can Start in Childhood

Watch little children play. See their joy: how they marvel at the beauty of a yellow monarch butterfly, laugh with gusto at a silly joke, give big bear hugs to strangers and friends, delight in telling you about their talents and successes, and aren't ashamed of a chubby tummy.

When did your Bitch steal this joy? She might have early origins, since genetics loads the gun with tendencies toward anxiety, depression, and obsessions, and life can pull the trigger at any age. So your insecurity and self-criticism might have started when you were too young to remember. On the other hand, you may vividly remember the time, place, and person that began killing your natural happiness and optimism.

So many things happen to a child that can stick in her mind as a Bitch; events that may seem completely insignificant to an adult. Playmates say or do cruel things; parents, coaches, and teachers lose their temper; and children witness upsetting things in real life or on TV. Any of these can have a lifelong effect.

For example, a woman who can never say "no" for fear of displeasing someone may have been a little girl whose parent yelled, calling her selfish when she didn't want to share her toys. Or her Little Bitch may have told her, "Your parents would never have divorced if you had been nicer." She may have pushed these events out of her mind, but the feelings have affected her all her life.

The main point is this: Almost everyone suffers from what psychologists call "calamities of childhood," things that make us fear losing love, health, or approval. It can be a casual remark or something more deliberately cruel. Whatever it is, it yanks our security blanket away and allows The Bitch to make us act needy, defensive, fearful, or distant.

To help you identify the calamities that started your Bitch, this chapter will explore some of the most common ways we become emotionally scarred from childhood through college.

FEELING DUMB

When you were in school, did you discover that there was something the other kids could do that you couldn't? Did something come easily to most of your classmates that you had to really work to learn? Maybe, no matter how hard you worked, you just couldn't learn or do something.

If this happened, you probably had some form of learning disability, some form of "mis-wiring" in your brain that affects the way you process, store, or produce information. While the estimates of how many kids have learning disabilities vary widely from 2 to 10 percent, my experience is that most of us, even the most intelligent of us, have something that blocks the way we read, write, learn languages or math, move, or sit still.

While boys tend to be diagnosed with more learning disabilities than girls, especially hyperactivity that keeps them from being able to sit still in the classroom, many girls are profoundly affected by these problems, too. All too often, even for a person who is very bright in many ways, if there is something she can't do, The Bitch starts telling her, "You're dumb." And, unfortunately, The Bitch always makes us more aware of our faults than our assets.

Here's an example of what happened to one little girl I'll call Kelly. While Kelly did well in school, math never came easily, so when she began to learn about multiplication, her mother made flash cards to help her remember the multiplication tables. But Kelly's best friend told her that smart kids didn't have to use flash cards—they just "knew" multiplication. Suddenly, the friend's words became a Bitch in Kelly's head saying she was stupid and could never learn math. Kelly became so math phobic, she had to be tutored through high school and college. But the tutoring worked, not just in overcoming Kelly's math phobia, but also in quieting The Bitch enough for Kelly to get an MBA and a job with a major consulting company.

Another girl had a second-grade teacher who had the children read a story in class and then write something about it that night. The girl could read well and she could write, so the teacher became infuriated when she would not turn in her homework. Several years later, when her parents had a psychologist test her to see why she was having so many problems turning in papers, tests revealed that she didn't have long-term memory for what she had read. But by that time, she had incorporated the feeling of being "bad," which led her to be angry and rebellious, especially when written assignments were due.

One woman told me, "I could never learn foreign languages. Everyone was quick to assume that I simply wasn't trying to learn Spanish or French. They thought I was just being lazy. Little did they know how hard I was trying. I really wanted to travel the world when I grew up and converse with people in their language. People always said, 'If you spend time abroad, you will just pick it up.' But I never could."

Every time I hear one of these stories, I can empathize strongly, because even though most learning came easily to me, I never learned my left from my right. My teachers thought I was intelligent, but my Bitch tortured me with, "How smart can you be if you don't know your left from your right?"

I assumed I was doing a great job of fooling people, making them think I was smart. But when someone gave me simple directions like "turn right" or "go in the third door to your left," I panicked inside and bumbled around, thinking that if I didn't guess correctly, they would discover I was stupid.

When I finally studied learning disabilities in graduate school, I learned how many smart people have these learning glitches. It was such a profound relief. I could finally tell my Bitch that just because I didn't know my left from my right, it didn't mean I was dumb.

BODY IMAGE PROBLEMS

When you were a little kid, did somebody give you a nickname that made you feel awful? Were you called Fat Face, Witch Nose, Señorita Clumsy Feet, or something else that made you feel ashamed? Many adults cringe when they look in the mirror or see old photos, still hearing those taunts echoing in their minds from childhood.

If by some miracle you made it through elementary school without being teased about your appearance, the horrors of preteen and teen life awaited you, as they did me. I had been the star of several elementary school musicals, not letting the fact that I was short and chubby stop me from trying out for—and getting—romantic leads. I had no stage fright. Singing, dancing, and performing were pure pleasure for me.

During the summer between sixth and seventh grade, my body completely changed. I was transformed into a tall, gawky string bean. But I never thought that my body type should keep me from starring in the class musical in seventh grade.

So there I was, up on the stage, happily auditioning until the new music teacher called out, "Jackie, why are you trying out for the lead? You're a head taller than all the boys!"

As everyone started laughing, a massive, bone-rattling stage fright descended on me. I felt huge and gawky. My Bitch began shaming me, saying, "You have made a complete fool out of yourself! Forget singing and dancing. If you ever even try to speak in public again, you will look like an idiot."

For years, I was too uncomfortable to speak in class, much less ever audition again. If I was called on and had to stand up and say more than a word or two, I would blush, stammer, and shake. The Bitch had created a self-fulfilling prophecy: I did feel like an idiot.

I successfully avoided all forms of public speaking until I realized— oh, my God—I have to defend my dissertation in front of a panel of eminent professors in order to get my Ph.D.

I had a choice: I could drop out of my doctoral program and let The Bitch continue to keep me fearful. Or I could try to be the kind of person I wanted to be: someone who overcame her fear of public speaking. I didn't know if I could succeed, but I was determined to try.

So I spent a year writing my dissertation and sampling every form of therapy I thought might help me overcome my fear: hypnosis, group therapy, behavior modification, relaxation, and desensitization. (You will learn more about how to use some of these techniques in later chapters.)

I discovered that symptoms like mine—stammering, blushing, and shaking—are high blood pressure symptoms caused by stress, not "idiocy." And as I carefully watched other people giving speeches, I noticed that even those who looked utterly self-confident had shaky hands as they began their talk.

I practiced and practiced talking about my research. My husband and friends peppered me with every question they could think of. Finally, for the first time since seventh grade, when I walked into the room to face the professors who would grill me about my dissertation, I felt relaxed and self-confident.

After that, I forced myself to keep giving presentations, first starting with small groups and working up to bigger and bigger ones. If I felt myself beginning to blush and stammer, I would simply smile and tell the audience, "Don't worry. I get a little nervous when I start a speech. It goes away." That undercut my Bitch, and it seemed that half the people in every audience nodded in empathy because they had public speaking phobias, too.

Finally, my childhood pleasure in performing returned. Now, I enjoy speaking to large audiences. But I will never sing or dance on stage again.

STICKY LABELS

Do relationships fall apart because people keep accusing you of behaving in a certain way? Have a number of people said you are cold, selfish, or defensive? If there is consistency to their negative feedback, it may be true. Your Bitch may be encouraging you to behave in ways that keep you from establishing close, loving relationships for fear that they could fall apart and hurt you. Why?

Possibly, when you were a child, your best friend dumped you and started laughing about you with her new best friend. Maybe a group of mean girls picked on you and made you the class scapegoat. Maybe the first boy (or girl) you had a massive crush on rejected you, calling you an insulting name. Even if in retrospect you realize how unimportant this was, your self-confidence probably took a hit. And that feeling may have lasted to this day. The point is that there are many ways your Bitch can make you distrust the old adage that it is better to have loved and lost than never to have loved at all.

Families can label one child "the stupid one," "the bad one," "the dumb one," or "the selfish one." Children should never be given such labels, but it happens—and it sticks. I have worked with beautiful women who still feel like "the homely one," and smart women, who despite earning graduate degrees, are still labeled "dumb" by their families. Unfair family feedback can become a Bitch you believe even when all the evidence indicates otherwise.

A friend of mine told me that her mother, in a voice dripping with sarcasm, once said, "Well, I guess you got the looks and your brother got the brains," when she brought home a poor report card. When my friend finally got the courage twenty years later to ask her mother why she had done this, her mother had no memory of the incident. She was probably just in a bad mood that day. But The Bitch had made my friend remember—and obsessively work to prove she was smarter than her brother—ever since.

FEAR OF INTIMACY

What if you know you act in ways that push people away but have no idea where it came from or what to do about it? In therapy, childhood fears are often uncovered through "transference," a fancy word that simply means that how the patient acts toward the therapist is usually how the patient acts toward the rest of the world. Or put another way, if The Bitch makes you think you can protect yourself against old fears and losses by acting inappropriately aggressive, distant, or passive, you are going to act that way toward your therapist.

Here's an example a prominent psychoanalyst shared recently: He was treating a stand-up comic who tried to make a joke out of everything, including how old and stuffy the analyst was. Most people would get annoyed and feel insulted, but therapists are trained to use their feelings for greater understanding. By repeatedly but pleasantly asking what was going on when the comedian got insulting, the patient finally revealed that the analyst reminded her of her grandfather, the relative who had provided the most love and stability in her childhood.

When her grandfather died, she was left feeling overwhelmingly sad, alone, and unprotected. Her Bitch began saying that if she made a joke of everything, and kept men at bay with her sharp tongue, she could protect herself from sadness and future losses.

IF SCHOOL, FRIENDS, AND FAMILY
DIDN'T GET YOU, THE MEDIA WILL

Even if you were always surrounded by a loving, supportive family, and only had kindly mentors and friends through school, the world could have put a Bitch in your head, especially in adolescence, when hormonal changes cause confusing sexual and aggressive feelings as well as embarrassing pimples.

You may have escaped being damaged by mean girls at your school, but no one escapes the meanness of the media that constantly says we should look like beautiful, airbrushed, super thin, professionally made-up teen models.

And if you were a kid in the 1990s or after, you may not realize that you were subjected to far more "adult" messages on television, radio, and in advertising than any other generation before. Television stopped prohibiting sex and violence before 9:00 p.m. MTV and radio played music with far more explicit and misogynistic lyrics. And advertisers like Abercrombie & Fitch and Calvin Klein featured overtly sexualized teens. Researchers found that this took away the protection that children needed, pressuring kids to drink, dress in suggestive ways, dislike their bodies, and have sex far before they were emotionally ready for it.

If you think you weren't affected, take a look at *Reviving Ophelia*, a popular book that came out in 1994, written by Mary Pipher, a psychologist who specializes in treating adolescent girls. Dr. Pipher writes that she began wondering why, when we were more intent than ever on raising assertive, self-confident girls, therapists' practices were flooded by young kids with anorexia, sexually transmitted diseases, and drug and alcohol issues. She says, "Junior high school seemed like a crucible. Many confident, well-adjusted girls were transformed into sad and angry failures." And she was seeing this in middle-class, Midwestern families.

Pipher concluded the kids were coming of age in a "girl poisoning . . . dangerous, sexualized, and media saturated culture. They face incredible pressures to be beautiful and sophisticated, which in junior high means using chemicals and being sexual." In other words, the media and The Bitch were pushing girls to act like adults well before they were emotionally ready. And, of course, boys were also being pushed to act too macho.

If you think this sounds prudish, you should know that many researchers are still saying and finding the same things today. The media were often an unhealthy influence on girls when you were growing up. And they are still pressuring young girls the same way today.

DID SUCCESS MAKE YOU FEEL LIKE AN IMPOSTER?

The Imposter Syndrome (originally called the Imposter Phenomenon) was first diagnosed by Dr. Pauline Clance, a psychologist who worked in a counseling center at a highly competitive college. English majors would come in and tell her that some terrible mistake had been made by Admissions, because they were not smart enough to be there. When Dr. Clance would pull up their records, she noted that their grades were fine. "Maybe I'm getting decent grades," the student would counter, "but the really smart kids who deserve to be here are the math majors."

Then another student would come in and report feeling the same way. But this one would be a math major, claiming that the really smart kids who *deserved* to be there were English majors. These kids had worked hard to gain admission to a prestigious school, but somehow they felt that they had faked their way into the small percentage of applicants chosen.

Since then, other researchers across the country have found the Imposter Syndrome is pervasive. For example, Caltech, one of the most prestigious and competitive universities in the country, found their smartest female students often felt like frauds.

The Caltech Counseling Center website states that a gifted woman often works "hard in order to prevent people from discovering that she is an 'imposter.' This hard work often leads to more praise and success, which perpetuates the imposter feelings and fears of being 'found out' . . . because she feels she is a 'phony' and a 'fake.'"

And the feeling doesn't end after graduation. Women with years of success behind them admit to having these feelings. In an interview in

2002, Meryl Streep said, "You think, 'Why would anyone want to see me again in a movie?' And I don't know how to act anyway. So why am I doing this?" Similarly Sheryl Sandberg, chief operating officer of Facebook, admits in her best-selling advice book for women in business, *Lean In*, that "I still face situations that I fear are beyond my capabilities. I still have days when I feel like a fraud. But now I know to take a deep breath and keep my hand up."

BANISHING THE BITCH

The joyful, confident child you once were is still inside you. That is your natural birthright. Perhaps your Bitch has buried the free, pleasurable approach to life deep inside. But as a psychologist, I can promise that you don't have to stay feeling like a scared, fearful child. You may have to dig deep inside your memories and psyche, but you can recapture a positive approach to yourself and life, and make it yours again.

Find Out When the Joy Left

Look at old photographs and see if you can detect when and then how The Bitch entered your head and began to sap your joy.

- Did you happen to be born to people who didn't know how to love, encourage, and support a child?
- Did some mean kid call you fat face? Or crooked nose? Smelly pants? Big butt? Were you humiliated by being picked last for the team?
- Did some "calamity of childhood" make you feel bad or stupid? Did you learn that your body was shameful—or the only reason a boy would like you?

If you know where your Bitch started in childhood, you can see that situation no longer applies to you as an adult. Just as you no longer believe in the bogeyman, you no longer have to believe what The Bitch told you. You are in charge of your life now and can make positive changes.

Talk to Your Inner Child

We all have an inner child that retains the fears and pain of childhood. Whenever your joy was poisoned, kind self-talk now can be the antidote. But we also have an inner child that retains the joyful, self-confident optimism of childhood—even if it is buried deep inside. Deliberately begin to search for the joyful part that was lost.

If something specific made you feel bad, try to either put it in the past or find a solution. For example, if you think that a learning disability made you feel dumb, the good news is that even now, if it is diagnosed, you can often be taught ways to compensate for it.

Psychologists have discovered that there isn't just one form of intelligence—there are many. And these various kinds of intelligence affect everything from our ability to read, do math, create art and music, or to interact easily with other people. So if there is something you could not do and your Bitch started calling you dumb, it's time to focus on what you do well, rather than what you don't.

Here's the point: We all have to act like good parents to ourselves. If you are saying something to yourself that you would never say to your child, it has to stop. Then you must become as comforting, nurturing, and healing as you would to a hurt child. Wipe insulting words out of your vocabulary and replace them with kind affirmations. This is called Cognitive Therapy, and here is the do-it-yourself version:

If you hear yourself say, "I'm stupid," counter it with something like, "I am not stupid; I simply don't know my left from my right." Turn "I'm an imposter" into "I must be competent because look how many other people think I can do the work." "No one will ever love me" must become something like, "I am loveable, and whoever made me feel the opposite was probably very screwed up."

Most important, counter any "calamity of childhood" with, "That was then, and this is now!"

Keep Up an Inner Dialogue

If you play hardball with yourself, you may have to have an extensive therapeutic internal dialogue, arguing with your Bitch as if she were a real person. This may sound crazy, but it is part of Cognitive Therapy and it works if you keep it up. Here's what it might sound like:

"I'm so stupid!"

"Just because you feel stupid, doesn't mean you really are. You got plenty of good grades."

"Yes, but the teacher just liked me because he thought I was funny and cute."

"It's true that teachers have their favorite students, but it's ridiculous to think that you fooled all your teachers into giving you good grades. And how about the promotion your boss just gave you? Doesn't that prove something?"

"My boss just gave me a raise because I needed the money."

"Your employer is not a charity: people are promoted because of what the employer needs, not because the employee is needy."

"But what about the time I didn't get the raise—or the time I got fired?"

"Even if it was your fault that you got fired, you can correct your mistakes and restart your career."

"But . . ."

"No buts and no Bitch crap! Knock it off! Now, let's go out and have some fun."

3

BEAUTY AND THE BITCH
Inner Ugliness

Body-image expert Dr. Rita Freedman told me that men and women usually act in different ways when they look in a mirror. "Even if a woman is young and beautiful, odds are she won't be pleased when she looks in a mirror. She will focus on the few things she doesn't like that day—the wrinkle on her forehead or the shape of her nose." That's all The Bitch will let her see. "But when men look in a mirror," said Dr. Freedman, "they tend to focus on the details they like and ignore what they don't."

A woman who ran a fashion business and traveled around the United States for seven years selling a line of clothing directly to customers told me, "I saw thousands of women standing in front of mirrors, and literally there was only one who seemed completely pleased with how she looked. Every one of the others made comments like, 'My stomach looks too big.' Or 'I can't wear this because of my neck.' Or 'I can never wear belts.'"

Why should this be? And why do even young women, who have taken Women's Studies and know lookism is toxic, still feel this way? There are huge corporate industries built around making women feel they need to improve their looks. How would the cosmetics, fashion, and magazine companies survive if we all decided we look just fine as we are?

And here's a great irony: women who decide they look fine as they are, but would also like to lose weight are far more likely to succeed with their diets than women who let The Bitch criticize their overweight bodies! That's one aspect of the Bitch-defeating psychology of beauty and health discussed in this chapter.

YOU LOOK FAT

If I had to pick The Bitch's favorite line, it's probably "You look fat." Although "How could you be so stupid?" is a great runner-up. And just as she tortures teens, saying, "Everyone is staring at the hideous pimple on your nose," she says the same thing about the bulges virtually every woman has.

That's why we all look at tabloids while waiting in supermarket lines. We see stars living out our Beauty Bitch nightmares: close-up pictures of cellulite as celebrities try to enjoy a day at the beach. Muffin tops popping out from $200 jeans become major news. And what about the analysis every time Jennifer Aniston gains a pound or two? Does it mean she's pregnant?

Usually these photos just feed our insecurities. But a recent spread in *In Touch* magazine allowed celebrities to give their comments about their imperfect bodies. I almost started cheering in the supermarket line as I read that Reese Witherspoon said, "I have stretch marks. I have cellulite. Your body never looks the same after you have children." But that wasn't going to stop her from having fun with her kids on the beach.

While Madonna's picture of sagging skin under her arms elicited the expected admission that she had a "love/hate" relationship with her body, other stars served as role models like Reese. Supermodel Kate Upton said she wasn't going to "starve just to be thin," even though she had some unflattering back fat. And when paparazzi caught Jennifer Lopez's tummy rolls during a workout session, she said, "There's nothing wrong with me or my shape," admitting that she likes to occasionally treat herself to a couple of cookies.

Magda Szubanski, star of the Australian version of *Kath and Kim*, allowed Jenny Craig to publicize her weight-loss campaign in 2008. As her weight came down fifty-five pounds, Jenny Craig memberships shot up 50 percent. But then Magda's pounds came rolling back.

In 2014, Magda reported on NPR's *The Moth Radio Hour* that one day she was about to spend some time on the beach when she spotted paparazzi waiting for her. "I was wearing my clingy bathing suit. I wanted to run away." But after a few minutes of indecision, she says she "decided not to play the shame game" and strolled onto the beach. Later, she tried not to mind when the pictures were published and the press started a public debate about whether she looked voluptuous or merely fat.

Magda also faced down The Bitch in another way: In 2012, she announced she was a lesbian. "I've always been very private," she told Sydney's *Daily Telegraph*. "But I think after years of doing therapy, and also as you get older you think: 'Oh, whatever. So I struggle with my weight? So what? I struggle with my sexuality. But that's life.'" Go Magda! That's the way to shut The Bitch up!

BEAUTY IS IN THE MIND OF THE BEHELD

Two of my first patients taught me that beauty is not, as the old saying goes, in the mind of the beholder. It's in the mind of the beheld. The two women were both blondes about the same age, but far different in appearance. Donna had a curvy, beautiful figure. Gina was so heavy, I worried every time she sat in the antique rocking chair I had in my office. Would it collapse into a pile of splinters?

Conventionally pretty, Donna complained she couldn't get a date. Why? Her Bitch made her so shy that she gave the impression that she didn't want attention. For example, when a man smiled at her, The Bitch said, "He's probably smiling at someone else nearby. You'll make a fool of yourself if you smile back." Or if a man said, "What are you doing this weekend?" Donna thought she would sound pathetic if she said, "Nothing." So she always said, "I have plans." As she sat alone on Saturday nights, she allowed her Bitch to convince her that this was further proof that she would never find anyone to love.

Gina had the opposite problem: how to choose between several boyfriends. I happened to know one of them, and he was a very attractive man.

Gina loved men and sex. Her sensual, flirtatious nature attracted men. This made her feel that all the Bitchy prejudice against fat people didn't apply to her. Of course, not every man found Gina attractive, but there were more than enough who did.

HOW TO GET RID OF THE "YOU LOOK FAT" BITCH

With all the hype and pressure about body image these days, how can you know the truth about your weight? For a dose of reality, go to the Centers for Disease Control and Prevention website (cdc.gov) and type in "healthy weight." That will take you to a place where you can calculate your body mass index. After you enter your height and weight, it will tell you whether you are underweight, normal/healthy, overweight, or obese.

If it says you are underweight, please believe it rather than The Beauty Bitch. Similarly, if it says you are overweight or obese, don't let The Bitch insult you or your body, but do take active steps to change. Being too thin or too heavy can damage your health and even kill you. So I strongly advise anyone who is not in the normal/healthy range to go to a doctor who will help you devise a wellness plan.

The next few pages contain tips for the vast majority of us who want to drop some weight, feel healthier, enjoy our bodies, and get rid of The Beauty Bitch who tells us we are too fat.

Focus on a Healthy Body

A thirty-two-year-old personal trainer from Connecticut, Bradley Wiedl, informed me that sticking to an exercise and nutrition plan can be more psychological than physical. "For people who are in decent shape and want to take their fitness to the next level, the biggest obstacle tends to be finding the time to make their health a priority. I had a female client, for example, who really only needed three to four hours a week of exercise. But she was so busy juggling husband, kids, mother, and home that she declared she had no time to exercise."

The Bitch makes women like that feel guilty about taking time for themselves, even if it's for their own health, putting them in a no-win position. If they don't work out, The Bitch says they look flabby. If they do work out, The Bitch says they are being selfish and "should" be doing other things.

On the other hand, Bradley finds that "people who have a lot of weight to lose are usually incredibly motivated and committed in the beginning. They are excited when they lose thirty pounds in three months. But when they inevitably hit a plateau, instead of pushing through, they get frustrated. Negative thoughts start derailing their program. They revert to their old habits, start skipping workouts, eating poorly and then have to start from square one again."

No matter who he is working with, home cooking can be the key to weight loss. "Restaurants are the silent killers, with everything loaded with butter, salt, and sugar to make it taste good. A main course can have 1,200 to 2,000 calories—that's a whole day's worth of calories. If you are trying to lose weight and you regularly eat out or order in, you are bound to run into trouble since you have no idea what you are actually consuming." And of course, The Bitch will blame you, not the chef.

Foster Self-acceptance

Dr. Rita Freedman, the body image expert I quoted at the beginning of this chapter, told me, "If a woman looks in the mirror and criticizes what she sees, she will feel less confident and, therefore, may be more likely to seek comfort in high calorie foods and less likely to stay on a healthy eating plan."

Self-acceptance can mean acting like a man and focusing on the things that you like about yourself when you look in the mirror—giving yourself a smile and a compliment. It means looking in the mirror and instead of saying, "You have all those ugly fat rolls around your waist," saying, "I would like to have a smaller waist, but in the meantime, I look pretty in this dress." It means not letting The Bitch berate you when you fall off your diet, but making a plan to avoid temptations in the future.

Reduce Stress

Okay. You know all about ordering a baked potato topped with plain yogurt instead of a bucket of fries. You know about sipping a decaf cappuccino while everyone else is indulging in dessert. And you are trying to love your love handles while you are also trying to get rid of them. So why can't you stick to your healthy eating plan?

John Kral, a physician at the State University of New York's Downstate Medical School, specializes in obesity and eating behavior. He told me that "stress drives a lot of women's over-eating."

Dr. Kral gave me two research papers written by others. The first compared 651 men to 620 women and found that women, especially young women, were more susceptible to stress at home and work. No surprise, I thought, as the image of a mother I know came to mind. She commutes to her job in Washington each day with pumps attached to both breasts. I hear a lot from women about their stressful multitasking, but her double breast pump commute tops them all.

But what does stress have to do with body fat? The second research paper, titled "Comfort Food Is Comforting to Those Most Stressed," confirmed what every woman knows: when we are stressed we reach for high-calorie food.

> "Here's the simple explanation," Dr. Kral explained. "The brain works on sugar energy. Stress fires up the brain and it sends a signal to the body to send it sugar. So the body begins craving high caloric food."
>
> I said, "What about those lucky women who say that when they are upset they can't eat?"
>
> "They are more prone to depression and other diseases like ulcers," Dr. Kral said.
>
> "Whew! Given the choice of being fat or having ulcers, what's a woman to do?" I joked.
>
> But Dr. Kral gave me a serious answer. "You know what Freud said about pain and suffering?" he asked. "Freud said to avoid them. I say the same thing about stress. Avoid it whenever you can."

Great advice, but given the work and family responsibilities that most women are shouldering, it's difficult. What we all can avoid, however, is the unnecessary stress The Bitch subjects us to. And we can be more mindful: When stress makes us want to grab a cookie, we can grab a carrot instead. Or, even better, we can go for a walk.

Learn Weight-Loss Tricks

Weight-loss tricks can empower and help you conquer The Bitch when she's making you feel bad about your weight.

Throw fattening food away before you finish. Delia Ephron wrote an essay about how she adores bakeries. And despite the fact that she often goes to several each day, she doesn't gain weight. Her secret? "Discardia—the tendency to throw things away after a few bites unless I fall in love. Thank God for Discardia, or I would be someone who has to be removed from my house with a crane."

I've never met a chip I didn't like, so I practice Discardia before I consume the whole bag. And just throwing them in the garbage doesn't work for me. I have been known to drag them out again. But running them through the disposal removes all temptation.

The Bitch will tell you, "That's wasteful!" Yeah, but she'll also torture you if you eat the whole bag or the whole piece of cake from the bakery. So save the calories and flip The Bitch the bird.

Take a day off. Here's the typical pattern: A woman stays on her healthy eating program for a week. Then cupcakes, ice cream, or a big wedge of Brie become too much temptation and she slips. But the overeating is nothing compared to the beating The Bitch gives her: "You fat slob, you'll never be able to lose weight." Or "You can never stick to anything. What's wrong with you?"

Why would you give yourself more grief about the one day of slippage than praise for all the days you stayed on the program? Why not just say to yourself, "I had a bad day" instead of "I'm weak and fat and bad and bloated"? Weight-loss programs that don't allow for occasional treats or "falling off the wagon" are unrealistic.

Some people who need structure and routine function best when they do not deviate from a strict program. But they especially need to shut The Bitch up when they fall off the wagon. Others are like a patient of mine who achieved a healthy body mass index and told me, "I decided to stick to a low-fat diet five days a week. Then I tell myself it's okay to eat chips and drink wine two days every weekend. I call those my Free Days, not my Bad Days." The point is, if it works for you, do it!

Act French. I always wondered how French friends could eat those fantastic five- or six-course lunches and dinners complete with wine and still stay slender. When I asked, they told me the secret: when they indulge in a huge lunch, they only eat a bowl of vegetable soup for dinner.

Consider Whether You Think You Are Benefiting from Your Extra Weight

There is a concept in psychology known as "secondary gains." Simply stated, it means that you will not overcome a problem if you are getting something out of it. And there are several ways that women may consciously or unconsciously think they benefit from being heavy.

It can be seen as a test of love. I know a twenty-year-old woman who was obese. No diet worked, so she had her stomach surgically tightened to allow less food to get in. With a smaller stomach, she also felt full after eating less. Even though this operation has a high success rate, she didn't lose weight. Why?

She told me that while she couldn't eat as much as she used to, that didn't make her lower her caloric intake. She discovered ice cream could slip through the smaller opening and dissolve as she crammed in more.

Why did she feel so miserable that she had surgery, only to deliberately "outsmart" it? Her Bitch was telling her that her family and men needed to prove their love by loving her despite her weight. When therapy helped her see that she was putting obstacles in the way of admiration, her surgery began "working."

A layer of fat can seem like armor. Another woman I know, Tina, had a different reason for staying heavy. Her Bitch told her that her extra weight was a protective shield. "It made me feel more substantial, more weighty. It made me feel I could stand up to people who were trying to push me around."

While everyone who knew Tina thought she was an assertive woman, her Bitch told her that she needed the extra weight to keep her bombastic husband from bullying her.

After Tina found the courage to leave her unhappy marriage, she started dating a slender man who loved her just as she was. Friends thought Tina was finally as fat and happy as one of those popular Botero sculptures, until she began losing weight. Feeling safe and loved, she no longer "needed" her fat as protective armor. She feels healthier than she ever has and just as assertive without the extra weight.

Weight as an anchor. My colleagues and I have noted that some women in unhappy marriages gain weight to anchor themselves to their spouse. Their Bitch tells them, "You better stay with your husband because you're too fat to attract another man," and they believe her. While heavy women like Tina and Gina prove this wrong, some women need an excuse to stay until they feel ready to go out on their own.

WHAT ABOUT YOUR FACE?

Just because I've talked so much about how mean The Beauty Bitch is to women about their bodies, don't think I've forgotten how mean we can be about our faces. The complicated relationship with facial mirrors can begin in childhood, when girls feel embarrassed over the idea that their cheeks are too fat, their nose is too big, or their teeth are too crooked. And if you get through childhood without those thoughts, don't you remember thinking that the whole world was staring at your zit?

And just when you finally stop getting zits, tiny lines begin to appear. The Bitch drives many of us to stare at the mirror every morning, wondering if those lines have become crow's feet.

In 2004, Dove soap launched its widely popular Campaign for Real Beauty with head-shot pictures of women who did not meet the norms for beauty set by women's magazines. The next year Dove moved on to ads featuring full-length shots of happy women displaying their "normal" bodies. The campaign was so successful that, in 2012, they tried a new tactic: hiring a forensic sketch artist to draw dual portraits of women—one based on their self-description and the other based on someone else's description. It should come as no surprise that women mentioned their "crow's feet, big jaws, protruding chins, and dark circles" far more than observers did.

Dove research found female self-criticism begins early all around the globe. Seventy-two percent of girls ten to seventeen years old said they felt "tremendous pressure" to be beautiful, but only 11 percent said they would use the word *beautiful* to describe their looks. However, girls had higher regard for their looks than women: only 4 percent of women would describe themselves as "beautiful."

What could make more women feel beautiful? I asked the owner of an expensive hair salon, a professional who looks at attractive women every day and goes home to one at night.

Here's what he thinks makes a woman beautiful and attractive to men: "Every woman has something beautiful about her—maybe her legs, maybe her eyes, maybe her smile. It is very attractive to men if she knows it and enjoys it.

"My job is to bring out and enhance her look, because confidence is the key to being beautiful and sexy. When a woman feels confident, you can see it in her eyes, her smile, and her body language. Maintaining eye contact is usually a sign that she is very confident in herself.

"The most beautiful women, however, are not necessarily attractive to men if they have a shell around them—a defensiveness that says, 'stay away.' They don't smile and they don't look you in the eye."

So while talented stylists can make a woman look her best, she won't feel beautiful until she stops letting The Bitch make her feel bad when she looks in the mirror.

BANISHING THE BITCH

While The Bitch seems to rear her head most when it comes to beauty and appearance, you can learn to ignore her and be content with who you are. A few of these tips may help:

Adopt a healthy lifestyle. Whether or not you aspire to be beautiful, aspire to be healthy. And don't lie to yourself about what that takes. Don't believe The Bitch if she tells you there is a magic supplement or pill or that you will get magic results simply by hiring a trainer. Understand the truth: Results come by integrating a healthy diet and exercise program into daily life. A first step might be learning to cook organic meat and vegetables. I can just hear your Bitch saying, "You don't have the time," and "That's too expensive!" So make a deal with yourself: Keep careful track for a week of the time and money you spend ordering in or going to restaurants. The next week keep track of the time and money you spend if you do some of your own cooking. Make simple things like broiled fish or chicken breasts coated with a little mustard and olive oil and green salad tossed with nuts, parmesan cheese, pepper, vinegar, and olive oil. You can eat for several days if you roast a chicken with vegetables.

Nicole, a twenty-seven-year-old woman in Brooklyn, works for a non-profit and can't afford to eat out every night like her friends who work in business and finance. "They probably can't afford it either, and their credit card bills are probably staggering, but that's another story," she told me. "Everybody thinks I'm a magician when I make a roast chicken or grill a steak. I mean, it's ridiculously easy to do those things and just throw some vegetables into the oven to roast or make a salad."

Both Nicole's body and bank account are healthy because she eats in often and has dinner parties. And she finds that giving a dinner party is no more expensive than taking herself out to a restaurant, since she asks her guests to bring the wine and dessert.

If you can't achieve a healthy body mass index, don't despair—seek medical help. Anorexia usually cannot be overcome without good medical and psychological help. The same is often the case with obesity.

The important point is that people who are obese shouldn't let The Bitch tell them that there is no hope. Dr. John Kral, the physician at Downstate Medical Center in New York, sees people who have tried many times to lose weight and are still clinically obese, sometimes two hundred to three hundred pounds overweight.

"Typically they have been through five to seven medically supervised weight-loss programs, but nothing has worked. They are discouraged by a trajectory of failure," says Dr. Kral. "The people I see have what I consider a disease that we now call 'diabesity.'" While there are many reasons why some people cannot control their overeating, regardless of whether it is genetic or otherwise, Dr. Kral says obesity can often be helped by surgical methods to alter the gastrointestinal tract.

When you look in the mirror, act like a man—or a smart woman. Smile when you look in the mirror every morning, instead of checking for "crow's feet." And when you look in the mirror before leaving the house, why make yourself miserable as you head out the door? Even if you think you are overweight, do what men do and focus on your best features. Give yourself a smile and a compliment. Leave feeling confident. Go out and have fun. You will feel friendlier, happier, more optimistic, and more beautiful—and more able to stay on a healthy eating and exercise plan.

4

BITCH OF A DATE

The Bitch Makes Three a Crowd

Dating involves competition, rejection, sex, body image, major differences between men and women, a lack of clear rules, and a ticking time clock. Whew! No wonder dating affords The Bitch so many opportunities to foster shame, embarrassment, worry, and depression. But as we all know, a great date makes it worthwhile.

This chapter will cover various phases and aspects of dating. The goal here is to help you know what you want at each stage of your life, and to go for it, despite The Dating Bitch who is always giving bad advice.

HOOKUPS

The main purpose of a hookup is sex, usually with someone you barely know. Some women find hookups liberating. They are at a stage when they don't want an ongoing relationship, but they do want sex. On the other hand, there are women who find hookups immoral or depressing.

The important thing to know is where you stand and what you want, so you won't let The Dating Bitch push you into things that aren't right for you. Or make you feel guilty about getting what you want.

If you post your profile on Tinder or other dating websites, you have to declare what you are looking for—a friend, hookup, or relationship. And you will get instant matchups with people who post the same expectations. That can make dating life a little less confusing than it was a few years ago. But the research shows a lot of women are unclear about what they want, so their Bitch gives them expectations beyond what hookups usually offer.

Here is what a woman in her late twenties, who definitely knows what she wants, thinks about hookups. Like many other women in graduate school or with demanding jobs, she is too busy to have a relationship but sometimes wants to have sex. "I can't spend all the time it takes for a relationship. I'm at a stage in my life where I just want to be free. I don't want to be tied down. I only have Friday and Saturday nights off. So I want to spend that time hanging out with my friends. If I happen to meet the right guy, I guess I would settle down. But now if I want to have sex, I just hook up. I think in a few years I'll get tired of living this way and want to get serious but not now."

That woman knows what she wants and is able to compartmentalize sex from affection. But many women can't do that, according to a major report from the American Psychological Association. It concluded that the hookup culture left too many women feeling "used," and many men feeling like guilty "users."

Hookups, usually defined as uncommitted sex with someone you barely know, are very common these days, and those who hook up start young. While the estimates vary widely, it appears that 60–80 percent of college students in North America have hooked up. And while women can be as sexually liberated as men, there is still a gender gap in morning-after reactions: about 80 percent of men and 60 percent of women say they are glad they hooked up; however, half of the women but only a quarter of the men also had some regret or disappointment.

Another survey, this one conducted in singles bars, found 32 percent of men and 72 percent of women said they would feel guilty about having intercourse with someone they just met. So why do women hook up if they know their Bitch is going to bother them the next morning? The majority of all hookups occur after people have had at least three drinks—so booze makes people do things they will regret. And then, the next morning, The Bitch berates them for it.

The American Psychological Association report on the hookup culture also found The Bitch tells participants that "everyone is comfortable with this, so you should be, too," leading women to engage in aspects of casual sex beyond their comfort zone. And the sex is often a lot better for men than women.

Research shows that women enjoy sex more when they are in a committed relationship, because they have the time and intimacy to tell their partners what they like. Too often, The Bitch makes women too embarrassed to tell casual partners what makes them feel good, so what they get is too quick to be satisfying. As one woman said, "There was just a lot of thrusting. I don't think he tried to satisfy me at all. He just fell asleep and left me staring at the ceiling."

But I've found that even men who care sometimes don't realize that good sex involves more than thrusting if they learned their sexual technique from porn movies. And, unfortunately, porn movies are the main place too many men get their sex education.

Even women who thoroughly enjoy the sex can be unhappy with hookups if they expect them to lead to permanent relationships. I have seen that situation often in my practice. Here's an example:

Bonnie loved sex. She had had a long and active sex life that revolved around a couple of bars in the town where she lived. But when she was ready to find someone to love, get married, and have kids, no one she knew at her regular bars seemed to consider her "wife material."

Bonnie realized she could always go to a bar and meet men, but whenever she walked in and saw other women there, her Bitch said, "*They're* all so pretty . . . Look how *they* know how to laugh and be charming . . . But if you talk a little dirty and act sexy, men will want to be with you."

Bonnie couldn't understand why the men she dated were initially passionate but always cooled. Even relationships that were more than one-night stands rarely lasted a month. She told me, "Men are just dogs."

Actually, most men are hunters. If they are in a phase where they simply want to hook up with no strings attached, they think that's all women who act like Bonnie want, too. But if they are at a point in their lives when they are looking to settle down, many go into their hunting phase, enjoying a chase and the thrill of the hunt. Or at least they look for a woman whose Bitch doesn't beat her down and make her think that the only thing she has going for her is her body.

I helped Bonnie evaluate what she liked to do besides go to bars to have sex. She had been athletic in high school, so she decided to take up tennis again and begin to read the sports section of the newspaper. Flipping through the rest of the paper, she became interested in politics, too. And she took a jewelry-making course just for fun.

Once Bonnie began to develop interests beyond going to her favorite bar every night, she realized there were things she wanted to share with a man in addition to her body, and her social life improved. She still liked going to bars, but she stopped going to the ones where she was known as the go-to girl for casual sex.

As soon as she started what seemed like a solid relationship, Bonnie stopped coming to therapy. But she called and left me a message recently, saying that she was happily married and expecting a child.

FINDING A RELATIONSHIP

You are ready to settle down. You want more than a hookup. But The Bitch might try to tell you that since relationships didn't work out in the past, you don't deserve to be loved. Or since there are so many younger and more beautiful women around, why would anyone want you? Or while everyone else has found someone, you are destined to be alone forever.

The Dating Bitch sells this load of crap to a lot of people, but I've never worked with anyone of any age who genuinely wanted a relationship with a man and didn't find one. *If* they like men, *if* they like sex, *if* they aren't desperate, and *if* they keep up a concerted effort until they succeed.

It's my experience that when secure men get a whiff of desperation, they run. No wonder. A desperate person is more interested in finding a port in the storm than love. Who wants to be just a port? Only someone whose Bitch has given them a savior complex—and that rarely makes for a healthy marriage.

But when The Dating Bitch makes your biological clock send screaming alarms, how do you keep from feeling desperate? It's all too easy to get depressed and just sit at home every night, drowning your sorrows in wine or ice cream.

I know this advice is easier said than heeded, but there's only one positive plan other than becoming a single mom: Make your life as happy and fulfilling as you can while continuing to look for a mate. Spend time with the people who make you feel good and ditch the people who don't. Develop activities and hobbies that take you out into the world, nurture you, and make you feel good. Develop a rich, whole life. The more content you become with your active, fulfilling life, the more you will probably attract someone who wants to share it.

But in some areas of the country—Los Angeles, for example—it is easier for The Bitch to make women feel desperate, no matter how fulfilling their lives are. Stacey Howard and Jacqueline Kravette run an L.A.-based website called Lovefabu.com, where they hear about dating issues all the time.

"People call Los Angeles 'the Bagdad of dating' because the city is full of so many beautiful women," said Jacqueline. "A lot of men think that unless they are with a Victoria's Secret model, they can do better. They are used to having their pick. It's easy for women to feel discouraged."

I asked what advice they give when the competition looks like starlets. Here's what Stacey and Jacqueline said:

First of all, you have to know who you are and what makes you more than a pretty face and beautiful body. You have a mind, personality, and interests to share with someone. As Jacqueline said, "If you only base your self-esteem on looks, you will have low self-esteem, because there will always be someone prettier, younger, or thinner. You don't want to be with anyone who isn't interested in you as a whole person. You want to get rid of the players right away."

How do you know who the players are? "Anyone who is texting or looking all around the room while you are having a glass of wine together, or someone who is noncommittal about setting up another date," said Stacey.

But where do you find good men? "If you want to meet men, go where they are," Stacey advised. "You're not going to meet them in the mall or the hair salon. Home Depot is a great place to meet men. Strike up a conversation asking about whatever they are looking at. Or consider that co-ed sports, like beach volleyball, soccer, or bowling, often attract men who enjoy the company of women. Or go to a sports bar with a girlfriend and meet new guys there."

Stacey knows there are great guys everywhere. She met her husband on a street corner when he was new in town and needed directions.

Their advice reminded me that women in New York City often tell me they have met good men in similar ways: by striking up conversations with shoppers in Bloomingdale's men's department and boating supply stores or by joining co-ed softball teams that play in Central Park.

In fact, I have a friend, Sandra, who dated men she met offering to share a taxi, riding in elevators, and smiling at someone passing by while she was sitting alone having dinner in a restaurant. She met her steady boyfriend in the lobby of her apartment building. She's not beautiful, but her big smile and friendly demeanor pulls in men like a magnet.

The women who run Lovefabu.com believe the same thing: an open, friendly, self-confident attitude is everything.

TWO MORE WAYS TO
BITCH-PROOF YOUR DATING ATTITUDE

In addition to the great advice Stacey and Jacqueline gave, here are two ways I help clients Bitch-proof their dating attitudes. The first is a "secret formula" given to me by a woman named Nora. She claimed, "I can make any man fall in love with me."

Of course I asked how, and she said: "If I see an attractive man, I look him in the eyes and smile. As I talk to him and begin to find out about him, I give him compliments, genuine things that I like about him. I let him know I find him very attractive, but I don't rush into sex. Most women I know are far more eager to give a man sex than compliments. That usually doesn't work."

Nora didn't know that her secret formula is a version of what a man named Dale Carnegie wrote about in one of the best sellers of all time: *How to Win Friends and Influence People.* His simple truth and "trick" still works today: when you meet someone new, instead of worrying about whether they will like you, figure out something that you like about them—and tell them. Carnegie said that everyone—no matter how attractive and successful—is longing for a compliment, longing for someone to see what is good about them. A genuine smile and a genuine compliment begin many a genuine relationship.

The second "trick" counters The Bitch when she tells women that men have all the control. I remind women that all the men who are on-line looking for relationships are applying for "the job" of being a mate. Women have the ability to accept or reject them, too. So make a list of the things that you want in candidates for the position of your mate.

After a woman makes her list, I suggest that she narrow it down to the six to eight things that are most important to her. That list will help her know the difference between settling and settling down.

One thirty-one-year-old I worked with was beating herself up about putting so much energy into a relationship that failed. I asked her to make her "must have list," and she began with four items that I think are great:

- smart
- funny
- chemistry
- wants to settle down

Before she even added other qualities, she realized her ex lacked two of the top four.

Why only put six to eight qualities on the must have list? Because everyone has some good qualities. So you can get stuck in the wrong relationship, not realizing the person lacks the things that are make it or break it for you.

Even if the things on your list seem strange or unnecessary to other people (or your Bitch), stick with them if they are vital for you. For example, I worked with a woman who had grown up in a wealthy European family. She told me she needed a man who wore suits with functional buttonholes on the sleeves. When I said that such suits could be bought for a guy who never had them before, she countered with, "Yes, but I will not be happy with someone who doesn't appreciate the quality difference."

Some people might think only a bad Bitch would make her care about buttonholes—something many women would find trivial. But she knew what was right for her. She had married someone who didn't share her appreciation for the beautifully crafted things and good manners that were part of what she grew up with. That was a big reason her first marriage broke apart, and she didn't want to risk another divorce.

The point is to know when it would be better to be alone than to be with someone you just aren't simpatico with, and to know whether a person is someone you could settle down with, not just settle for. Equally important is to stop trying to hold on to someone who really doesn't love you. Don't ever allow The Bitch to convince you that you will never find someone else to love.

DITCH SOMEONE WHO ISN'T AS SERIOUS AS YOU WANT

Here's a classic joke that describes a mismatched couple:

Jim and Martha are driving in a car, when Martha asks Jim if he realizes it is the six-month anniversary of their first date. Silence ensues. Martha begins agonizing about how Jim is probably feeling pressured by her comment. Jim is thinking: Six months have gone by so fast! I bet my car is way overdue for an oil change.

Jim looks worried. He is concerned that any damage to his car will not be covered by the warranty. Martha notices his expression and agonizes more, thinking she has pressured him about the relationship.

Martha begins to cry, blurting out that she's a fool. Jim has no clue what she's talking about but bumbles into saying something nice.

Later at his house, Jim watches a football game between two colleges he has never heard of and goes to sleep deciding he will never figure Martha out, so he better not think about it. But Martha gets on the phone with her friends, and they begin a discussion of all the possible nuances of the situation with Jim; this conversation lasts for weeks.

This is a perfect example of a woman who wants a serious relationship but is too afraid to ask her boyfriend if he wants that, too. Martha should feel entitled to say, "We've been going out for six months, and I'm really happy. But I'm wondering where this relationship is going." The Bitch should not make her afraid to ask this, or afraid that Jim might indicate the relationship isn't going where Martha wants it to.

A sad Bonnie Raitt song tells a truth no lover wants to hear: "I can't make you love me if you don't." But The Dating Bitch makes it hard for a woman to accept that if they love someone deeply, he might never love them back. Unrequited love plagues people with thoughts like: Why, why, why doesn't he call me? . . . I must have done something wrong . . . There must be something I could do to get him back.

These thoughts go round and round in a person's head, sometimes becoming so obsessive that it's hard to think of anything else. Then The

Bitch encourages unhelpful things like driving by a beloved's house to see if he is home, or to see if some other woman is there. The next step might be making lots of calls and hanging up, or regularly checking his Facebook page to see if he has listed himself as single or posted pictures with another woman.

And if there are pictures of another woman, that can start a whole new obsession: Who is she? What does she have that I don't? Maybe if I just wait around, he'll get tired of her and come back to me.

Forget it. While a man who leaves his wife for another woman often comes back, a boyfriend rarely does. So, looking to replace an ex is no-lose. If you find someone better (even if The Bitch is telling you there is *no one in the whole world* who is better than him), that's great. If you find a substitute and Mr. Wonderful wants to come back to you, you will be in the control seat, deciding if you want him or not.

BANISHING THE BITCH

Finding love can be tough, and The Bitch has many ways of exploiting that insecurity. She can make you feel that you don't deserve to be loved or that you don't have anything to offer a prospective mate except sex. If you are in an unhealthy relationship, she can make you feel that no one else will ever love you, keeping you stuck. You have to ignore her and have the confidence to pursue what you really want and not settle for anything less. Some of these tips may help:

Be honest with yourself about what you want. Have a serious conversation with yourself when The Bitch isn't listening. Do you want to just hook up or do you want a relationship? If you want a relationship, are you ready to settle down? If you are ready to settle down, how does the guy you are with score on your checklist of things you must have in a mate? Get rid of shame if you just want to hook up—or if you want to ask for commitment.

Understand that dating is like a casting call and lots of people audition. Just as you have probably been unable to love a number of men who are perfectly nice and good looking, it's the same with some men who meet you. You just weren't their type. Or they have commitment issues. Or they wanted someone shorter, blonder, or less assertive. But there are loads of guys who want someone tall, brunette, and strong. So if, as they famously say on *Sex and the City*, "He's just not into you," keep looking for someone who is.

If you are not using online dating sites, you are not seriously looking. If The Bitch is telling you that only pathetic people go on those sites, check some out and you will find that men and women of every socio-economic status use them. *US Weekly* published a list of stars who have used online dating that included Adele, Halle Berry, Orlando Bloom, Ashton Kutcher, Britney Spears, and Martha Stewart. I have personally known psychologists, physicians, executives, and men who were on the boards of major museums who found their mates on dating sites.

Why do even highly successful people need to go on the web to find a mate? For the same reasons you might: they exhausted the list of people they and their friends knew, and they were uncomfortable dating someone at work for fear it could go wrong and get ugly.

And here's a great benefit: with all the specialized dating sites, if there is something unusual that you must have in a mate, it's likely that you will find that special someone online. For example, I bet you can find people who hate meat or love cats as much as you do. You can probably even find a European with real buttonholes on his sleeves.

5

BITCH AND CHAIN

Divorce The Bitch Instead of Your Mate

And they lived happily ever after. Well, only in fairy tales, no matter what The Bitch and Walt Disney say. In Disney movies, the heroine finds Prince Charming, who is flawless and always adoring. In real life, there are no such men. But let's face it; none of us are adorable, ever-cheerful Cinderellas, either.

Even so, we can have happy marriages, as long as we avoid The Marriage Bitch who works in two opposite ways. On one hand, she tries to convince some wives to put up with genuinely bad behavior, even abuse. On the other hand, she exaggerates some men's flaws to such an extent that it breaks up what could be a good relationship.

Ideally, everyone who marries knows their partner well, and they have participated in some type of premarital counseling so they know whether they agree on key issues like money, religion, sex, children, chores, and obligations to family, friends, and work. But time changes people and expectations, so even if the couple was sublimely happy and congenial before the wedding, The Marriage Bitch can quickly make sweet turn sour.

But here's the good news: after working with many couples over the years, I have found that if both partners want to save a marriage, it can almost always be repaired. However, there is one exception.

Can you guess what that exception is? Infidelity? Alcoholism? Terrible sex? No. All of those issues can be overcome. But when respect is gone, the marriage is dead. So beware: if you start to think your partner is "a child," "stupid," or "worthless," watch out.

This chapter will cover some of the issues that often arise in marriage counseling. You will find that while the issues seem different, a common theme runs through all of them: they can all be solved by negotiation. But The Bitch escalates problems when she blocks fair give and take.

EXPECTING PERFECTION

Here's a terrible joke someone sent me from the Internet: The Five Rules for Men to Follow to Have a Happy Life:

1. Have a woman who helps at home, cooks from time to time, cleans up, and has a job.
2. Have a woman who makes you laugh.
3. Have a woman you can trust and who doesn't lie.
4. Have a woman who's good in bed and always likes to be with you.
5. Never let those four women know about each other or you could end up dead.

Why do I include this silly joke? To make the point that no woman or man is perfect. We all have wonderful qualities and we all have terrible flaws. The question is: Which flaws can you live with? But The Marriage Bitch tells us to expect perfection and often compares a spouse to an overly idealized lover or father, causing marital strife.

For example, I worked with a couple I'll call Marian and Frank, who had unrealistic ideas about marriage. The Bitch told Marian, "Look at Tina's husband. He stays home the whole weekend and plays with the kids instead of being selfish like Frank!" So Marian made Frank's life miserable because he wanted to spend Saturday mornings biking with his buddies.

Frank was a good husband and father, who deserved a few hours of fun. Marian's constant complaints—"Why are you out biking when you should be home with the kids?"—just made Frank want to stay away longer. He would promise to be home by eleven, but "somehow" never show up until noon. While Marian stewed and watched the clock, The Bitch berated her for being "stupid" and marrying a "selfish" man.

But Frank had some Bitch-fueled ideas, too. He had gotten his sex education by watching porn, so his Bitch called him "stupid" for marrying a "cold" woman who didn't like oral sex. How could he think that calling Marian cold would make her feel hot?

Every day, therapists see couples like this. The only things that differentiate them are the issues they fight over. As Tolstoy famously said, "Happy families are all alike; every unhappy family is unhappy in its own way." The Bitch creates resentment, anger, and defiance, making each partner feel not just hurt, but self-righteous.

I asked Dr. Gloria Kahn, a colleague of mine who specializes in marriage and group counseling, how she would begin to deal with a couple like Marian and Frank.

"The place I would start is their lack of compassion for each other, their lack of understanding how the other feels," Dr. Kahn said.

"I would ask Marian how she feels when Frank doesn't come home when he says he will. She will probably say, 'angry.' But I will push her to talk about the hurt behind the anger, because expressing anger evokes a spouse's anger, but a spouse can usually be compassionate about the hurt.

"Marian would probably say something like 'When I'm waiting for you and it's past when you say you'll be home, I get upset because I think you don't care about me. And that makes me angry.'"

Couples get themselves locked into angry arguments by accusing the other of what therapists call "you" statements: you did this, you did that, you are an idiot! This just causes the other person to feel angry and defiant.

But by getting couples to use "I" statements, to only talk about their own feelings when certain situations happen, their partner can often hear what is going on in a way that can be negotiated and changed.

Dr. Kahn would ask Frank to repeat back what Marian said to be sure he heard and understood correctly. Then she would ask how he would feel if Marian kept him waiting all the time.

As for the couple's sexual impasse, Dr. Kahn says she would begin by explaining the rule of thumb that therapists apply to sex: Do whatever feels good to *both* partners. If it doesn't feel good to one spouse, they have veto power.

"As for oral sex, some women love it and others hate it. And some are fine with it as long as it doesn't involve ejaculation, because that makes them feel like they are choking. So, I would explore with Marian where she stands and see if there is some comfortable compromise she can make."

If Marian is in the "hate it!" group, then Dr. Kahn would explore with Frank what makes oral sex so important to him. Is it the submissive/master aspect? Does it make him feel that Marian is taking care of him? Or is it the fact that she is in control?

"Whatever his desired feeling, I would assure him that there is nothing wrong with that," says Dr. Kahn. "Then we would try to find a way to satisfy him that is comfortable for Marian. For example, if he wants Marian to be in control, maybe he would like sex where she is on top. Or if he would like her to take care of him, perhaps she could use her hand instead of her mouth."

The point is, whether it's sex or any other of the typical issues couples fight about—money, religion, relatives, or parenting, for example—marriage counselors try to encourage couples to work on understanding the feelings, so they can find a solution or compromise.

WANTING TO WIN, NOT COMPROMISE

By the time most couples come for marriage counseling, they are furious with each other. Their Bitch tells them it would be "weak" to compromise. In fact, she says that compromise or negotiation would be letting their spouse get away with bad behavior. So each person wants the therapist to tell their spouse, "You are very bad and have to do exactly what your spouse wants!" While that might be gratifying to one person, it won't create a permanent peace. But when the therapist mediates a compromise that pleases both parties, the marriage is saved.

I learned a simple technique for this from a divorce mediator in San Diego, and I firmly believe that if couples used this approach together at home, they would save a lot of money on therapy and divorce lawyers. Here's what the mediator told me, "I sit down with the couple and let each of them tell me how the situation seems to them. Instead of letting them fight about their different views, I get each of them to calmly state how they see the conflicts and what they want. Then—and this is the real switch in the brain when mediating disputes—I say, 'Can you think of a solution that you can accept that your partner might go for?'" It makes people think in terms of compromise and win-win solutions. It defeats The Marriage Bitch who always thinks in terms of win-lose and makes spouses believe they were "stupid" to marry someone so imperfect and obstinate compared to others.

But there are many situations in a marriage that really are win-lose. I want to go to the mountains on vacation; you want to go to the beach. I want to spend extra money on a new sofa; you want to spend it on a pool table. I want to move to Hong Kong; you want to stay in New York. I want to have sex right now; you don't.

In happy marriages, couples adopt solutions like, "You win this one, and I get to win the next." Or they let whoever feels the most passionate get their way. But in unhappy marriages, one partner feels the other *always* wins.

I remember working with a couple, Carol and Bob, two attractive, strong-willed people who each adamantly claimed that the other always won. When I pointed out that this was impossible, they refused to back down. So I proposed a simple solution: Post a calendar on your refrigerator and from now on, mark down who wins each conflict. Both partners were amazed to see what the other thought of as a "win."

When Carol wanted Bob to go shopping with her on Saturday morning, but he went out to play tennis, she marked this on the calendar as a win for him. When she made arrangements to have dinner with a couple he didn't particularly like, he marked that as a win for her. No matter if Bob said, "You know I don't like to go shopping," or Carol said, "Yes, but we owe that couple a dinner date," the person who felt like the loser got to mark it on the calendar.

At the end of a month, it was clear to both Carol and Bob that they had a relatively equal marriage. The calendar showed the facts, so they could no longer fight about who "always" won. For couples where the calendar reveals that things are genuinely unequal, the partner who is being pushed around has the facts to renegotiate the marital balance of power.

NOT SHARING ASSETS AND POWER

These days, couples often start off as equal partners, with an equal say about everything from where they are going to vacation to what kind of furniture they are going to buy when they move in together. Typically this state of happy equality lasts until the baby arrives.

Then it is not uncommon for the wife to cut back her working hours or become a full-time mom. And The Bitch can begin to make her feel like a very unequal partner.

When I first started my practice, I was amazed to see how quickly many women lost their sense of self-confidence when they quit their job to stay home with children. Women who once were dentists, television producers, or corporate executives listened to a Bitch who told them they were "nothing" without their job.

Many told me they dreaded going to parties for fear that someone would ask, "What do you do?" Their Bitch told them no one would want to talk to them if they said they were "just a mother."

But their relationship with their husbands changed, too, as The Bitch told them, "He earns the money so you should do what he wants." A friend of mine who had been a top salesperson once told me, "It's his money so he should say how we spend it." It seemed like she was literally shrinking as her self-esteem drained away.

"Well, actually," I said, "it's not his money. He may get the paycheck, but according to most state laws, as his wife, that money is yours as well as his."

Marriage counselors often use another way of defeating The Bitch when she tells you that the money is his: They monetize the value of the homemaker. Write down all the tasks and responsibilities that the stay-at-home person completes. Then ask how much you would have to pay a person to do this.

How much would you have to pay to have someone come at 6:00 or 7:00 a.m. to get the kids ready for school? How much would you have to pay for a personal chef and shopper? How much would you have to pay for someone to chauffeur your kids to school and activities?

And here's the big economic contribution: How would the primary breadwinner function if someone was not taking care of the kids? The old movie *Kramer vs. Kramer* (1979) is still absolutely relevant: Dustin Hoffman can't keep his demanding job in advertising when Meryl Streep leaves him and their little boy to function on their own. Rent the movie from Netflix if you want to see how a loving, caretaking parent is crucial to the success of a hard-driving professional.

NOT SHARING RESPONSIBILITIES

If both partners continue to work full time after they have children, unless they have a lot of household help, there is simply too much to do. Resentment creeps in as the couple begins to fight about who should do what. And The Bitch always says you are an idiot for having married someone who is unfair, selfish, and acting like a child.

Psychologist and author Carin Rubenstein found that even if financial responsibilities are fairly shared these days, household tasks still are not. While that's been true for decades, Rubenstein discovered that modern husbands are now claiming incompetence: "You load the dishwasher so much better than I do" . . . "I don't know how to diaper the baby" . . . "When I try to cook, I burn everything." While this may be an excuse to get out of work, it may also be The Bitch making them feel inadequate.

Obviously, husbands can learn to do household chores, but The Bitch tells wives, "You are the woman, so you should be doing the housework," or "It's easier to do it yourself than challenge his ridiculous excuses." However, this eventually leads wives to feel, as many have told me, "He's so unhelpful, it's like I've got another child instead of a husband."

This is obviously bad for wives, but can you guess why it's bad for husbands? Wives lose their sexual desire when men are unhelpful. How to get desire back? The Cambridge Women's Pornography Collective put together a funny, but all-too-true book, *Porn for Women*, which shows handsome men doing things like cleaning the stove before they are asked.

But porn is always unrealistic fantasy, isn't it? So here's what therapists suggest overworked, overstressed couples do:

- Make a list of all the household chores that have to be done.
- Knock off any chore that is superfluous, or can be done less often. For example, do you really have to make the beds? Do you have to dust or vacuum more than once a week?
- Knock off chores that can be outsourced. Does the budget permit cleaning help? Is there a service in town that washes and folds the laundry? Can the babysitter (or the college kid next door) be paid a little extra to make a simple dinner every night for the whole family?

- Have each spouse choose whatever they don't mind doing from the list.
- Divide the heinous things that are left in an equal manner.

WHEN TO CALL IT QUITS

Divorce is one of the most difficult decisions you will ever make, even more difficult than whether to marry. And the day your divorce becomes final, even if you were looking forward to it, The Bitch will probably call you "a failure." But sometimes, no matter how painful, it is the best decision.

Pamela, an African American in her late forties, had a rich, full life revolving around her job, her church, and her family. "I am the oldest in a family of seven," she told me. "I have plenty of nephews and nieces, so I didn't miss having children. But I've taken care of other people all my life, so as I got older, I longed for a companion, someone who would take care of me sometimes.

"I prayed and prayed for a man to come into my life, but when I turned forty, I decided my prayers were not going to be answered. Then I met a new man who joined my church, and he seemed wonderful. He was so interested in everything I did and so helpful to me. I felt God had finally answered my prayers.

"But the day we married, everything began changing. He stopped being loving. He started to criticize me and slowly he became abusive. I was confused. I kept asking: Why is this happening? Why is this man who acted so wonderful now acting so bad? I was so embarrassed that I only told my priest and one of my sisters what was going on."

Pamela didn't want to tell me the specifics about how abusive her husband was or what the main issues were. It really doesn't matter because The Bitch should never convince a person to stay in a marriage that feels abusive. But to answer her "Why?" questions, here are some reasons men change right after marriage:

- The Madonna/Whore Syndrome: If a man suddenly stops wanting to have sex after marriage, he might feel that it is okay for a girlfriend to be sexual, but a wife (especially if she becomes a mother) should be "pure." And in this kind of distorted thinking, "pure" means asexual.

- Girlfriend versus Housewife: In some men's minds, this is another big difference between a girlfriend and a wife. While he never expected a girlfriend to cook, clean, or wait on him, suddenly he expects his wife to handle these household tasks.
- Classic Abuse Syndrome: Since Pamela mentioned the word "abuse" and her priest didn't object to her leaving her husband, I have to assume that this was the problem. A classic abuser is charming and loving until he is sure he "has" the woman. Then he slowly begins to isolate and criticize her. (See more about this in Chapter 14, "The Bitch in Someone Else's Head.")

Whatever the specific misery that Pamela was suffering, her priest agreed that she had grounds for a separation. But her Bitch made her too insecure, embarrassed and self-blaming to act on that advice. "It took me two years to ask my husband to leave," she told me. "My priest called the next day and said, 'I'm not going to ask you to stay together. But I am going to ask you to stop asking why. Instead, I want you to ask, 'What is the lesson I must learn from this?'

"My lesson was empathy. Before this, if anyone had told me they would stay with an abusive man, I would have been very judgmental. But I had stayed for two years."

If you are in a similar situation, try to seek outside help, because The Bitch can easily erode your self-esteem and make you believe that you deserve bad treatment and have to stay. She might convince you that you are simply overreacting or cause you to believe that no one else will ever love you. But remember, people who don't treat you well don't practice real love. An outside, objective person, such as a therapist, can help you ignore The Bitch, recognize that you deserve to be happy, and move on to a healthy relationship.

BANISHING THE BITCH

Marriage takes work and compromise, but it can be even harder when The Bitch is always in your head, making you doubt your choice of spouse or feel powerless when you are not the main breadwinner. The good news is that once you identify The Bitch in your head, you will recognize this voice when you hear it, be better able to ignore the negativity and handle your issues in a more rational, loving manner. The following tips can help:

Create a no-insult zone. Your home should be a safe refuge where people are loved and accepted. Of course you are going to be annoyed or angry sometimes, but it's vital to discuss problems in a way that excludes insults to you or anyone else in the family.

I have worked with many spouses who grew up in homes where insults were the norm. They hated it, but somehow when frustration set into their own marriages, they found themselves continuing the tradition. It's not okay. You don't want your kids to grow up and insult their kids and spouse. Dysfunctional family traditions have to stop with you.

Believe it or not, you can make stopping insults a fun family game: If anyone is caught insulting someone in the family, they have to put a dollar into a piggy bank. If kids don't have the money, they have to forfeit part of their weekly allowance—or a treat they want. But when the piggy bank is full, the money is used for a family outing.

Be giving, but only give what your spouse wants. There is an old saying that in a good marriage, each party thinks they are giving 60 percent. But the sad truth is that many people who give a great deal get no thanks because they are giving what *they want*, not what their spouse wants. So if your Bitch says there is something wrong with you because you give and give, but get no appreciation, perhaps you are giving the wrong things—or to the wrong person.

The book *The 5 Love Languages* explains that different people want to be given different things in a marriage: words of affection, quality time, gifts, acts of service, or physical touch. You and your mate can take a quiz at fivelovelanguages.com to see the best things to give each other.

If you have to divorce, get support to make it civil. As I said at the beginning, most marriages can be saved if both parties want to work at it. But even if respect is gone and the marriage is dead, that doesn't mean the couple should divorce if they don't want to. Here's a quick rule of thumb to determine if "staying together for the kids" is The Bitch talking or rational thinking: a couple should not live together if there is abuse, or if the relationship is so toxic that it would damage children.

If you do decide to divorce, never let The Bitch convince you to use the kids as a weapon. Unless one person is a bully, use a mediator rather than a killer lawyer: go for win–win solutions. But if your spouse hires a killer lawyer, you will probably need therapeutic as well as legal support.

6

THE PARENTING BITCH

Give Her a Time-Out

People have become parents since Adam and Eve, so how hard can it be? That's what I thought as my belly grew so gigantic that it looked like I might explode. I was about to start my Ph.D. in psychology, so I was sure that common sense augmented with psychology would make me Supermom. But as the old saying goes, pride cometh before a fall. Within months, my Supermom cape was in tatters.

I'm pretty calm by nature and I was being trained to keep cool even when dealing with a suicidal patient. So I was shocked to discover that when my adorable baby cried all night, night after night, I understood how parents could get so crazed that they throw their kid out the window.

When I couldn't comfort the baby, The Bitch would say, "What's wrong with you? Maybe you're too tense. Maybe you just don't have 'a mother's comforting touch.'"

Then, as the cries continued, the message was "Maybe something is dreadfully wrong—call the doctor, call the hospital!!" I argued that Bitch down, but when the crying lasted for hours, and no amount of soothing, walking, and rocking—not to mention feeding and diaper changes—calmed the baby, I would begin to get frantic. Luckily I had a husband I could wake up and say, "You take over," when I was at the end of my rope. But I couldn't sleep because The Bitch was telling me what an awful mother I was.

It gets easier as your children get older, right? Sometimes. But the day after my five hundred fellow therapists presented me with their Distinguished Psychologist award, my two kids, who usually played nicely together, were screaming and fighting so much that I found myself jumping up and down and yelling. Stopping myself in mid-shriek, I was mortified. The Bitch screamed, "If any of your colleagues could see you now, they would rip the award off your wall!"

Why am I revealing these embarrassing truths? Because I bet almost everyone who tries to be a good parent has similar tales about almost really losing it. That's why The Bitch finds such fertile ground with parents.

Motherhood allows most of us to discover a depth of love we never knew existed—plus a greater depth of guilt, too. And if we don't guilt ourselves, there are plenty of other people who will try to do it for us.

So this chapter will start with maternal guilt and how The Bitch tries to convince you that you are not a good mother. Then it will discuss an innate factor that can't be changed: temperament. Next I will discuss three key aspects of personality that a parent can shape in order to avoid instilling The Bitch in her child: kindness, self-discipline, and resilience. Finally, since a parent who wants to foster self-discipline and resilience has to let the child struggle and fail, the chapter will end with guidelines for when to step in and help a child and when to give yourself a time-out.

A CLASSIC RECIPE FOR MATERNAL GUILT

Start with crazy expectations. You want to be the best mother in the whole world. As Joyce Maynard wrote, "I thought it was a mother's job to make her children's lives as perfect as her own had failed to be."

Exaggerate mistakes. When one teacher let her precocious sixteen-month-old play with a jumpy-toy labeled "for three and up," he fell off and hit his head. As she comforted his wails, she imagined the headlines, "Educator Indicted for Murder of Child!" She repeatedly told all her friends, "I'm a horrible mother!"

Add plenty of judgment from the outside world. A professor said she felt judged by the "mythical mother's court" because she did not breastfeed her baby. I thought she was being overly sensitive, until I met adoptive moms who told me they were criticized for not trying to breastfeed.

A mom in Portland told me about the pressure she gets to feed her child organic food. "Can you imagine how guilty I feel because I can't afford to do this all the time?" she asked.

And while moms all over the country find social media helps with tips, it also shares harsh judgments over things like pacifiers, sleeping in the parents' bed, and whether to let your child cry. But here's the most extreme case I heard: A woman on the West Coast told me that when her friend vented frustrations on Facebook about her two-year-old, a local DJ picked it up and labeled her a "terrible mother." She received so much hate mail that she had to threaten a lawsuit to get the harassment to stop.

Accept as valid all the pressures put on mothers, not fathers. For example, when a woman recently ran for governor of Texas, the media questioned how she could handle her two children plus that job, but no one asked the same about her male opponent.

Blame the father if he doesn't feel as guilty and pressured as you do. Research shows that men and women can react differently to parenthood. For example, when women hear a baby cry, MRIs show that part of their brains snap to attention, but that doesn't happen for men, suggesting that many fathers have to be trained to be responsive.

Similarly, a colleague who specialized in researching and counseling fathers once told me that if I wanted to know the difference between mothers and fathers, I should look at how they handle a baby. Mothers cradle the baby close to them, while fathers throw the baby in the air. I will bet that no mother reading this book has ever tossed her baby to the ceiling.

My colleague said this shows that a father's role is to help the child become independent while the mother's role is to keep him safe. While clearly an overstatement, this is the basis for many parental arguments and a lot of maternal guilt.

Stir all together, sprinkle with a little perfectionism, and bake under pressure. Let The Bitch serve you a big portion, make you clean your plate, and ask for more!

IT IS DIFFICULT TO CHANGE
A CHILD'S TEMPERAMENT

In groundbreaking research, two psychiatrists, Stella Chess and Alexander Thomas, followed over a hundred children from birth into their twenties and concluded that everyone is born with one of three temperaments that can be roughly described as easygoing, shy, or difficult.

Similarly, Tracy Hogg, author of the popular Baby Whisperer series, describes five different kinds of temperament.

Many psychologists acknowledge the importance of a child's temperament but see it in a less formal way. For example, Dr. Suzanne Reiffel, a psychologist in Scarsdale, New York, and co-creator of Tool Kits for Kids, products that help children build resilience and self-esteem, describes temperament in children as having many different shades: "Temperament doesn't have to fit into pre-determined labels. Rather, it can be seen as an array of many emotional styles. Each child has a unique set of emotional characteristics that contribute to his or her temperament."

But whether there are three or five or an array of temperaments, here are some facts almost all professionals agree on:

First: It is innate, meaning temperament can be observed from the day you are born. Scientists and parents can see how adaptable a baby is to change and the baby's ratio of good to bad moods.

Second: Temperament cannot be changed, but some aspects can be modified. For example, shy or grumpy children can be slowly and gently taught to be more adaptable, but they probably are not going to become easygoing.

Third: It lasts through life. Temperament is not something a child will grow out of.

Parents give themselves a lot of credit if they have an adaptable, easygoing child who has more good moods than bad. But The Bitch makes parents blame themselves (or each other, or the child) if their child is the shy and fearful type or the grumpy, irritable type.

I start with this research to show that no matter what your Bitch says, while parents have a great deal of control over some aspects of their children's lives and personality, there is also a great deal that is out of a parent's control. The nature versus nurture versus society debate will go on forever, but here's the truth: it's all three. And the nurturing requirements vary depending on what kind of child you happen to give birth to. Don't let The Bitch blame you for your child's temperament.

HOW TO RAISE A CHILD WITH
KINDNESS INSTEAD OF THE BITCH

Recent studies have found that all around the world, what parents want most in their child, even more than achievement, is caring. Here's the good news: caring is a quality that is very much in a parent's control. But ironically, much of what the latest "experts" and The Bitch tell you to do does not produce empathy.

A major task of parenting is to teach a child how to be an empathetic, caring person. To do this, parents need to let children know what constitutes good behavior and what doesn't. For example, a parent might say, "Good for you. You shared your toy," or "I like how you helped your brother." Although some parents may overuse the phrase "good job," praise is essential to help structure a child's sense of what is good behavior and reinforce it.

Parents can help create empathy and helpfulness by guiding children through their interactions with other children—explaining how the other child might be feeling and offering possible solutions to problems that may arise.

The Bitch can creep in when parents say things like, "Bad girl! You shouldn't have done that," or "That was selfish!" A small child might start to feel bad about herself, believing that her mom and dad think she is bad.

Instead, it is important to separate the behavior from the innate value of the child. For example, the parent could say, "You did a bad thing. Let's try sharing this time." By helping the child see that she is a good person, but has done a bad thing, she will be much more ready to learn and internalize the good behavior because she is not feeling bad about herself. And The Bitch will not have a chance to grow.

Adam Grant, a professor at the University of Pennsylvania who has written extensively on the subject of morality, kindness, and helpfulness, encourages parents to express disappointment in bad behavior, rather than harsh judgment. He writes, "The beauty of expressing disappointment is that it communicates disapproval of the bad behavior coupled with high expectations and the potential for improvement." Just as Mr. Rogers communicated to children on his highly praised PBS show, Adam Grant proposes that we say to children, "You're a good person, even if you did a bad thing, and I know you can do better."

When teaching your child to be kind and caring, don't let The Bitch make you passive when it comes to expecting your child to treat you kindly, too. I have watched in horror as parents allowed their children to hit them and kick them, without an effective "No! That hurts."

I remember a very sad session I had with a woman who had tried all her life to be a good, kind, and supportive mother. Her twenty-three-year-old daughter who lived in another state had not bothered to call or send a card for Mother's Day.

In tears, the woman told me, "I thought kindness bred kindness."

"Only when lack of kindness is not tolerated," I replied.

By never insisting that her daughter treat her nicely, this mother had unwittingly raised a very selfish person. The daughter's behavior on Mother's Day seemed less of an oversight than typical behavior that the mother had tolerated since childhood. So don't let The Bitch make you feel guilty about wanting to be treated well by your child—or anybody.

YOU CAN HELP CREATE SELF-DISCIPLINE

About twenty years ago, educators around the country began noticing a strange phenomenon that still exists today: Parents don't want to say no to their children. As one woman who ran a nursery school in Pittsburgh told me, "When both parents work, they spend so little time with their children that they only want to see their kids smile."

But The Bitch tries to convince even stay-at-home moms that "Good parents never make their children unhappy" or "In happy homes, like the one next door, the children never cry" or "Don't get into arguments—if you die tomorrow, that's all your child will remember about you."

Actually, kids *need* to be unhappy sometimes. Why? Several reasons. First of all, children need to learn what's called "delay of gratification." In plain language, you can't always get what you want when you want it. Kids who don't learn this lack the self-discipline needed to succeed in school and work.

The second reason is that undisciplined children rarely get the thing they *really* need: genuine parental love and approval. It's hard to like a bratty kid, even your own.

But here's the good news: Parents don't always need to be strict disciplinarians, always saying no. Ann Kirkham, a beloved former nursery school teacher and mother of four kids, shared her methods for avoiding unnecessary fights:

"Kids need structure and a routine. They like knowing what to expect when they have a set schedule," she said. "When they are little, it makes them feel secure to know that there is a set dinner time and evening routine. The schedule that worked best for me was dinner, followed by a bath, brushing their teeth, and then a story before bedtime.

"I can understand why some parents just want to let their kids run around until they get tired, but it's too stimulating to play like that before bed. I've seen those kids in school and they are sleep deprived. Instead of having a fight every night when making the transition from play to bedtime, put a positive spin on it. For example, you could point to the schedule or the clock and say, 'Let's clean up the toys so I can read you that story we've been talking about.'"

I learned the same lesson when my kids were older by posting an outdoor temperature schedule I created: Depending on the temperature, the schedule said whether they had to wear a sweater or a coat, or not. I learned this technique from a book about negotiating; when rules are written down and posted, even adults tend not to argue about them.

"If there is a fussy night and the child doesn't want to follow the schedule," Ann advised, "give two choices that are fine with you: Do you want to brush your teeth or put on your pajamas? They get to feel they have some control and either choice works for you."

The Bitch might make you think all this stuff about schedules and choices is just too controlling. But it makes children feel secure to know that their parents are in control, doing what is best for their health and development. No matter what The Bitch says, you know more about what is good for your children than they do. Your child won't always like it, but he or she will benefit when you take charge.

Ann Kirkham says that too often parents feel guilty if they don't give their children a lot of choices, but that's too confusing for kids. Two choices, both of which are good for you, works in most situations. For example, if the child doesn't like what you made for dinner, they can choose cereal.

YOU CAN HELP CREATE RESILIENCE

Years ago, I interviewed a number of parents who had adopted special needs children and found that they had a lot to teach the rest of us. At first, I thought they were heartless as I watched their children hobble across the room to get their prosthetics or spend painful minutes putting on their shoes. But the parents explained the rule social workers had taught them: Don't do for your children what they can do for themselves. The children must learn to live in a world where you can't always protect them and do everything for them. It is kinder to let them struggle and learn to do things for themselves.

I have thought of those brave, kind parents so often over the years as I listened to teachers tell me how far parents go to do things for their children. For example, one nursery school teacher told me that a little boy in her class had never learned to put on his coat. When the mom saw that all the other little kids were putting on their own coats, instead of realizing it was time for her child to learn, too, she got angry at the teachers, saying to them, "Since all the other kids don't need help, you have the time to help Tyler put on his!"

If she keeps listening to The Parent Bitch, she will probably become one of the infamous "helicopter parents," well-meaning people whom The Bitch convinces to do their children's homework and fight all their battles. What's wrong with that? The kids never learn the value of resilience and hard work: how to pick yourself up from failure and work until you achieve success.

In Hong Kong, the current crop of children being raised by overly doting parents, grandparents, and nannies, are called The Strawberry Generation, because the kids look attractive and healthy but are squashed by small amounts of pressure. If your Bitch convinces you to be overly protective, saying that you are mean when you let your child struggle, get frustrated, and even occasionally fail, you could raise a Strawberry, too.

When to Step In

How much frustration should a parent allow? When should we step in and protect? Those agonizing questions are what make parenting the most difficult job I know.

A friend of mine, a yoga and fitness instructor, had a child who came home each day saying how much he hated school. He would squirm and cry and use any excuse to get out of doing his homework.

"I tried everything to help him, but nothing worked. I was really fed up," she told me. Her Bitch was making her feel frustrated and helpless.

"Then I had to take a course in metrics as part of a fitness certification. It was a four-hour class, and it felt impossible to me. Everyone else got it, but I just couldn't learn the material. I was squirming and watching the clock and all I could think of was how much I hated it and wanted to get out of there. Suddenly I realized that must be what my son was feeling."

She had him tested for learning disabilities and found he had some problems. She was able to send him to a school that specialized in helping such kids. "Very soon he started coming home and saying, 'It's so much fun to learn things!'"

No surprise that her Bitch started beating her up about not catching her son's problems earlier. But as I told her, none of his teachers or his father realized what was going on either, so she should be proud that she figured out how to help him. Now, after two years, he has transferred back to his old school and is doing fine.

The point is that any time your child is acting difficult, having a very bad time in school, or having a sudden change in personality, it is important to check it out. There may be some interpersonal or learning problem. And with older children, drugs or alcohol may be involved.

And while there is a legitimate debate about whether to let older teens drink at home so they will learn about alcohol before college, there is no such debate about drugs. Most of my colleagues who work with parents and teens say that there is a limit to privacy if you are concerned about drugs or weapons. All bets are off, and you can search your child's room if you think dangerous things like drugs or weapons are being hidden there. Don't let The Bitch make you feel like a snoop; check to see whether your intuition is on target.

TIME OUT FOR YOU AND YOUR CHILD

For little kids, a simple, loving way to discipline your child is a time-out: having your child sit in the corner or go to his room until he cools down. I think it can be equally important for over-stressed parents to give themselves time-outs, too. At the very least, walk away and literally count to ten. Don't let your Bitch make you feel guilty about needing a break.

The Allegheny Department of Human Services in Pittsburgh has found that just a small break and a kind word help defuse parent-child situations that could turn ugly. So they have trained grocery clerks and others to gently intervene when they see, for example, "a harried mother who has to grocery shop after work and lost patience with her child or a man who allowed his daughter to stand in the grocery cart."

If a bystander just says something like, "It's really hard to be a parent, isn't it?" to the harried mom, she can usually feel understood, take a breath, and calm down. Or if the dad hears something like, "Kids always want to do dangerous things like stand up in the cart, don't they?" it gives him the clue and courage to get the child to sit down.

The program in Pittsburgh is called "One Kind Word." And that's what all parents have to give themselves much more often.

Most parents lose it if they try to be with their children 24/7. But all too often, moms feel guilty about needing a break. (Yes, I said "moms." Dads don't seem to feel the same guilt if they want to go to the gym, have a beer with the guys, or play a round of golf or tennis on the weekends.)

Melissa Duclos is a mother of two who lives in Portland, Oregon. She gave me permission to quote from a wonderful article she wrote for *Cleaver Magazine* that talked about the Bitch-induced guilt a good mother can feel when she wants to take a break.

"I work from home, with the help of a part-time nanny," Melissa wrote. "She leaves in the early afternoon, and then I'm on my own with the kids until my husband gets home from work. My work, as a freelance writer, editor, and online writing instructor, is done almost entirely via e-mail. There are many days when I don't leave my house or talk to another adult outside of my own family. On those days, Facebook feels like my only link to the outside world."

But Melissa feels guilty when she frequently checks her phone, "not because I am ignoring the kids. I'm a firm believer that kids need to be ignored so they can learn to entertain themselves . . . I feel guilty because the phone tricks me into thinking I am alone when I am not, because it takes my mind out of the room in a way that dicing an onion for dinner or folding tiny socks does not. I feel guilty because I enjoy it. The sub-text of course is that I don't enjoy the time I could be spending with my children, or at least not as much. This is sometimes true and so I feel guilty for that, too.

"Checking Facebook on my phone makes me a terrible mother because it means there's something I'd rather be doing than building a Lego tower with my children. There's more, of course. I'm also a terrible mother because I am teaching my children that this kind of behavior is acceptable."

Whew! The Bitch is sure roasting Melissa for simply being human. Why shouldn't she give herself breaks? Why shouldn't she and her children sit together in the playroom for a while when she says, "You play with your Legos, while I play with my phone"?

Moms who work outside the home have lots of ways of letting The Bitch roast them, too. I remember reading that Mairead Corrigan Maguire, who won the Nobel Prize for leading peace marches that brought Catholics and Protestants together in Northern Ireland, said that when she was home with her kids, she felt guilty that she was not in her office promoting peace, but when she was in the office, she felt guilty that she wasn't home with the kids. What mother hasn't felt the same?

And here is a common variation on that theme: A manager at a major American bank told me how guilty she felt because she was going to take a job in a more family friendly European bank. It would give her more flex-time to be home with her baby, but The Bitch told her she was being a wuss, not putting her career first.

BANISHING THE BITCH

The Bitch really knows how to stick it to moms. Because our children are so important to us, it's easy for her to make us feel guilty about not spending enough time with them or make us question our ability. And, unfortunately, there is so much judgment when it comes to parenting that we often feel inadequate. Chances are, you are doing your best. And even if your child is having challenging moments, that doesn't make you a bad mom. Try to ignore The Bitch when she starts comparing you to other moms. If you raise your daughter with love, she will be better able to ignore her Bitch when she grows up, too.

Here are some tips to remember to help keep you sane and combat that self-critical voice:

Know that if mom isn't happy, nobody's happy. So, to the extent that your life and budget allow, work the way that makes you happiest and give yourself some personal time off. If your budget only permits child-care when you are at work, form a babysitting co-op with other parents. After an occasional lunch with a friend or a date night, you will come back much happier to spend time with your child. No matter what The Bitch says, even the most adoring moms need time off for themselves—preferably a little every day.

Give yourself a support group. And make sure it isn't a Bitchy one that makes you feel guilty about raising your child the way you feel is best. Online groups are fine, but nothing beats sitting around the play-ground or the playroom, sharing a cup of coffee and confidences with other mothers while watching the kids have fun together. Try to find like-minded, non-judgmental mothers—someone who criticizes your parenting decisions will only make The Bitch more prevalent.

And being friends with your teen's friends' mothers is just as helpful in a different way. For one thing, you can check when your teen says that "everybody is allowed to do it," whatever "it" is.

Even great kids are bad sometimes, and even great moms lose it. Everyone knows about the terrible twos. But did you know that even the nicest kids can turn snotty around eleven? But that doesn't mean you have to let them be snotty to you. And did you know that when teens can act their most unlovable and snarly is when they are in desperate need of parental love and control? Whew! No wonder we all need a few kind words.

7

THE BITCH AT WORK

How Not to Get Promoted

Jill, a young clothing designer in Los Angeles, had to face her Bitch after an up-and-coming actress bought one of her dresses and wore it to an awards event. When the photographs went viral, Jill was called for an interview with a top-level clothing company run by a designer whose name you would know. The first interview went very well, but, fearing failure, Jill told the company's human resources director that the job was too much of a stretch for her. While she had managed a small staff, she was afraid she didn't have enough experience to manage a large department.

Research shows that a man in Jill's situation would tend to take the position, assuming he would learn on the job. But The Bitch convinces women to look at success and failure in the opposite way from men.

When women fail, their inner Bitch says, "Dummy—you blew it," but when they succeed, The Bitch says, "You were lucky!" Men think the opposite: When they fail, men tend to blame the situation or someone else, but when they succeed, men take credit for being smart and competent. This Bitchy double jeopardy for women—no credit for success but all the blame for failure—makes women like Jill afraid to take risks. "I don't want to be one of those female managers everyone hates," she told me.

Again, her Bitch was just stirring up unfounded insecurities, because she would probably have a better chance of being liked than a man who took the job. That was the finding of a large study of almost twenty-five hundred managers in four hundred organizations in nineteen states: women are perceived by their coworkers—both male and female—as better managers than men.

The author of the study says that women managers effectively use skills such as communication, feedback, and empowering other employees. They are also skilled in decisiveness, planning, and setting standards.

Male managers were found to "still rely on a more autocratic style, emphasizing individual accomplishment and competition."

But The Bitch undermines career self-confidence in many ways, so this chapter will walk you through different aspects of work, from the interview, to relationships with coworkers and bosses, to handling stress and competition. Most of the information relates to people who work in offices, but the chapter ends with a work area that is particularly prone to Bitch stress: the arts.

BITCH-PROOF THE INTERVIEW

One of my clients, I'll call her Callie, had been looking for a job for a long time and went to a convention, hoping to make contacts. There, just as she had hoped, Callie met the head of an organization who seemed interested in her. This CEO looked at her resume, gave Callie her phone number, and said, "Call me." When Callie told me about this, I thought, "Bingo!"

But the next week, Callie had not made the call. "Oh, she was just being polite. She doesn't really want to hear from me," Callie said.

"CEOs might be polite, but they wouldn't give you their direct line if they didn't want to hear from you," I countered.

Callie told me she would call. But she didn't. The next week, she claimed, "By now she won't remember who I am."

I countered with, "What do you have to lose?" This worked. Callie called and was invited in for an interview.

But, as you probably guessed, Callie was in a panic because her Bitch told her she would blow the interview. So I gave her some tips that I give all job applicants, since everyone gets nervous before an interview:

Write five reasons why you would be good for the job on a file card and keep it in your purse or pocket. As you sit, waiting to be called into the interviewer's office, your Bitch is sure to try to torture you with something like, "They have so many applicants, why would they want me?" When she starts this self-defeating message, pull out your file card and read the reasons why the interviewer should hire you.

During the interview, make sure you work those five reasons into the conversation, selling yourself with a smile. Be prepared for tough questions and don't let anything the interviewer says throw you. If the interviewer seems rude or difficult, assume you are getting what is known as a stress interview.

Here's an example of a stress interview: Emma was trying to make a transition from a non-profit into the corporate world. She had good experience and transferable skills, but she was having a hard time convincing interviewers that this was so. Finally, she was called back for a second interview, this time with a top manager, but it seemed to go badly from the start.

He started with a gruff, "I can't see why Human Resources asked you to come back. You don't have any corporate experience."

But Emma had been studying her file card, so she wasn't thrown by that. She explained the skills she could bring to the corporation.

Then the manager noted the charity where she worked and said, "But you worked for a charity. I'm sure people there don't work as hard as we do here."

Emma was offended, but didn't show it. Instead, she pleasantly but firmly explained that people in her organization were very dedicated to their jobs, and she was certainly willing to work as hard as the people in his company.

"Whatever," he said and continued on with a few gruff questions about her salary and aspirations.

When Emma told me about the interview, she was steaming mad. "I would never work for someone like that!" she said.

But when the manager left the interview, he told Human Resources, "I don't care who else you are looking at. Hire Emma!"

It turns out, he was just giving Emma a stress interview to see if she was someone who could deal with difficult people and situations, someone who had the tact and self-control the position required. Emma got the job, and the man who interviewed her became her mentor.

Even if you don't have a stress interview, many of the questions you will be asked are stressful, especially if they want to know about the reasons you left other jobs.

Norma, a talented computer software expert, consulted me because while her resume attracted many job interviews, she never snagged a job offer. She concluded that she interviewed badly. And that was true. She got defensive, resenting interviewers' probing questions, because her

Bitch whispered, "Why are they asking *that*? They must think there's something wrong with you!" Norma's Bitch told her everyone was like her father, whose questions were intended to elicit information he could criticize rather than understand.

Once Norma and I practiced how to answer questions in a positive way, she received a great job offer.

REPLAYING FAMILY DRAMAS AT WORK

As a psychologist as well as a career counselor, I literally wrote the book on this one, *Divorcing a Corporation*, because I kept hearing how many patients felt compelled to re-create their unhappy family situations in the office. My book describes how intelligent men and women can act like children when confronted with bad bosses and coworkers. Here are a few examples:

You would think that a person who grew up with a very critical parent would do anything to get away from a mean, undercutting boss. Not so. The Bitch often traps them in what psychologists call "repetition compulsion," the perceived need to act out the situation that hurt them in childhood in hope of triumphing this time around. Somehow they think this will heal old wounds and set the problem right. It's the same reason children of alcoholics often marry alcoholics. It might sound reasonable, but it rarely works.

An information technology expert named Denise had an overly critical mother who never praised her. When I met Denise, she was stuck in a job that was well beneath her skill set with a demeaning boss to boot. When Denise described her boss, here's what she said, "Joan is just like my mother. If I can win her over, then I can do a lot of other things. If I just don't let her get to me . . . If I can only get through to her . . ."

Just as Denise could never win her mother's approval, she wasted valuable energy on an impossible ambition: winning over a boss who couldn't be won. But through therapy, she was able to disengage from this self-destructive task. She changed firms with an increase in pay to work for a boss who acts like a good mother, not a bad one.

There are many other ways The Bitch keeps us replaying unhappy family dramas at work. Do you know someone who is constantly jousting with colleagues? Hard-fought sibling rivalry can be replayed at the office when The Work Bitch encourages political battles that can harm careers.

I also discovered that the longer you stay at a company, the harder it is to leave. Even if you are unhappy, The Bitch tells you that the devils you know are less frightening than the ones you might encounter someplace new. After spending about eight years at a company, it can become so much like home and family that, even if it's an unhappy home and family, leaving can feel almost as traumatic as getting a divorce.

When people think they are crazy to feel so afraid to leave a job they dislike, I tell them that's why I titled my book *Divorcing a Corporation*.

TRYING TO KEEP UP WITH THE BOYS

The Bitch makes many men in many fields play the game of "mine is bigger than yours." Unfortunately, The Bitch and some bosses tell women if they want to be equal, they have to play by the same testosterone-crazy rules as the men. This phenomenon can reach its apex on Wall Street where the game can be played not only in terms of who makes the most money but also who works the longest hours.

WNYC, the public radio station in New York City, recently did a study on how much people sleep. One of their reports, "A Look at Sleep Deprivation, Wall Street Style," was chilling. No matter what time it is, markets are always open somewhere in the world, so trading has become a twenty-four-hour phenomenon. The reporter interviewed young traders who get up at four thirty in the morning and work all day and into the night fueled by lattes and energy drinks. He reported that young bankers brag about how little sleep they get, as if this were a badge of honor. The Bitch tells them that only wimps need six to eight hours of sleep each night. But after about four years of sleep deprivation, people begin to have emotional and physical breakdowns.

The combination of too little sleep and too much stress means people start making mistakes. And when they make mistakes, they often lose millions—and then have screaming breakdowns smashing their computers to bits.

But here's the saddest story I heard about trying to keep up with the boys on Wall Street. A friend who was a banker had a colleague who came back to work two weeks after giving birth to her third child. "She clearly was not well. She looked awful. I told her she should take more time off or at least go to the doctor, but she said she was afraid she wouldn't be respected by the men in the office if she did. Fatherhood was not a big priority in my department, and no one cut any slack for motherhood. It turned out she was hemorrhaging. She collapsed, and by the time she was taken to the hospital, it was too late. She died. I left the field after that."

Many consulting companies also expect their people to be on call twenty-four hours a day. One woman with an MBA told me, "I would work very late all week, and then on Sunday night, I would often get an e-mail at 9:00 p.m. telling me to rework material for a Monday morning meeting. I don't know how my fiancé fell in love with me," she said. "I was either working, sleeping, or crying."

Even though she was promoted and on her way to a successful consulting career, she decided the pace was killing her. Her Bitch tried to tell her she was a wuss when she switched to a company that had more sane working hours and expectations. While she makes less money, she has what she really wants: both a career and a personal life.

ASKING FOR A RAISE

All the research on male versus female pay shows that men still make more than women. Here's one reason: The Work Bitch makes many women afraid to ask for money.

The best time to ask for money is usually right after you receive a job offer. You know the employer wants you. They have told you the salary. Now is the time to see if there is any flexibility in that salary or in the benefits. There are many stories of new hires making more than people who have been in the job for years. It isn't fair, but if you don't ask, you often don't receive.

A former bank executive who teaches negotiation skills recently said this in an interview on NPR, "What I've found over time is that when it would come to bonus time, I would hear from the gentlemen,

'I want to make X.' I don't think I ever heard from a woman who worked for me, 'I want to make X.' And research shows, men ask and women don't."

She gave the example of having two employees who were each up for the same bonus. If the man comes in and asks for more, to keep him happy, he will probably get bumped up, which leaves less for the woman, since the bonus pool remains the same.

Why are women less comfortable asking for money than men? No one knows for sure, but one theory is that they are afraid to disrupt the relationship with their boss. Another is that many women are not as comfortable with the possibility that their request will be rejected. Remember the research I quoted at the beginning of this chapter—how we blame ourselves if we fail.

There is the old saying that the squeaky wheel gets the oil. And while that is often true, if The Bitch tells the wheel to squeak too loudly or too often, the wheel just gets replaced. It's unfair, but in many situations, if a woman uses the same tone and phrasing as a man to "squeak," she is labeled pushy, demanding, or a bitch. That's why mentors and women's support groups can be so important in coaching women about "the ask."

GET THE TRAINING YOU NEED

A successful executive who became a professor at the University of Pennsylvania told me that many academic women who are promoted lack the necessary management skills. The smart and secure ones get training through books, courses, or mentors. But too many others adopt a rigid, defensive "I'm right, you're wrong" mentality and resist hiring people they think might be smarter than they are.

I have seen that fearful attitude in many other fields, especially ones like information technology, where knowledge is changing so fast, it's hard to keep up. Managers often have young workers with greater knowledge and fresher skills working for them. The Bitch tells defensive bosses that they will look stupid or weak if they admit they need to learn new things. So they try to hold on by their fingertips instead of getting the training they need—either through courses or by asking their underlings to help them understand some of the new material. Bitch-free women are not afraid to ask for help.

THE ARTY BITCH

While some celebrities make millions, the vast majority of people in the arts are wildly underpaid—if they are paid at all. And The Arty Bitch rages constantly.

Almost every actress has a story. They go to a casting call all charged up only to find a hundred other women waiting to audition. Their agent says a director is looking for someone who is just their type, but then the director changes his mind and doesn't want that type at all, or wants someone younger. They finally get a big break—but their part is cut from the movie, the play closes after only a few performances, or the television show never airs. It's depressing and it's very hard not to take it personally. No wonder The Bitch is notorious for making actresses insecure.

But women in other areas of the arts are also attacked by The Bitch. As a photographer told me, "Expectations always have a way of outstripping skill." What she means is that the photographs she is pleased with one year look unprofessional the next year as her skills grow. The Bitch always points out the flaws in her work, so she never finds herself able to simply be proud of what she has done.

"When I go to a museum," said Kate Love, a painter who has been exhibited in the United States and Asia, "if the artist is really good, I tell myself I'll never be that good. But if the work is something that I think isn't as good as mine, instead of pumping me up, I tell myself that they were at the right place at the right time, and I'll never be that lucky."

This artist is hard on herself in other ways, too. "I can never rest on my laurels. I do the crossword puzzle every day and have gotten to a point where I can do the hardest ones: the *New York Times*' Saturday and Sunday puzzles. But after I give myself a nanosecond of congratulations, I want to push myself to see if I can do it next week in less time. I read that Bill Clinton can do the Sunday crossword in thirty-two minutes and I am nowhere near that."

When I told Kate about my Bitch research, she got it. Eyes wide with recognition, she said, "I've got to try to catch myself when my

Bitch makes me too competitive and back off—just try to enjoy myself and do a good job. If you live by superlatives—always having to be better than everyone else—you'll never be happy."

BANISHING THE BITCH

The Bitch in the workplace repeatedly holds us back, convincing us to accept less than we deserve out of fear. And when we do work up the courage to apply for a position we really want, she makes us insecure during the interview process. Learning how to eliminate The Bitch can do wonders for your career—both in asking for the raise and promotion you know you deserve and in moving on and finding something better when it's time. The tips below will help you get started:

Take credit for your success and don't be afraid to ask for more. Self-esteem and self-confidence are built by absorbing compliments and giving them to ourselves, not by attributing success to luck. Can you imagine a man who has just been told he did a great job, demurely shaking his head and saying, "Oh, I was just lucky"? Of course luck plays a part in every man's and woman's success, but so do hard work, skill, intelligence, and putting oneself in the right place at the right time.

I have heard that Margaret Thatcher once said, "I wasn't lucky. I deserved it." Perhaps the better truth for all successful people to say when complimented on their achievements is "Thanks so much. It feels great. I worked really hard for it."

Decide what you want next in terms of salary or promotion. Practice with friends or in front of a mirror saying what you want and why your work, contributions, and skills justify this.

If work isn't making you happy, change it or yourself. Maybe it's a vestige left over from our Puritan founding fathers, but centuries later, I still find people who think work should not be fun. All entry-level positions have a lot of unpleasant grunt work, but if you can't foresee a time when a promotion up the ladder leads to more pleasant tasks, begin looking for another job.

No matter what your field or level, if you have to force yourself to get out of bed each morning to go to work, something is very wrong.

Don't let The Bitch tell you everyone hates their job. That simply isn't true.

If you are replaying unhappy family dramas at work or if you feel stuck in the wrong field or the wrong profession, career counseling can help get you unstuck.

Break the stress habit. Constantly checking your BlackBerry or phone and working extremely long hours is unpleasant and exhausting, but it becomes a habit that's hard to break. People literally get addicted to the adrenaline rush, the stress, and the feeling that they are needed and important. Real life begins to seem dull by comparison until the habit is tamed or broken.

If you are not able to take the time for a personal life, or if you can't get seven to eight hours of sleep every night, something is very wrong. Reexamine your priorities to find a better work/life balance.

If you are chained to your BlackBerry day and night, proclaim some "off hours." If you can't give yourself a free hour with your family or friends without checking messages, again, something is very wrong, no matter what your Bitch says. Schedule forty-five minutes with your phone or BlackBerry off, and then check it for fifteen minutes. Turn it off again for forty-five minutes before you turn it on again. Addictions and bad habits can be broken.

8

SPORTY BITCH

What Makes Athletes Lose

There's nothing like having a strong and responsive body that reacts naturally and beautifully while playing a sport. Winning feels fantastic. And the pain of losing can be turned into a great lesson if The Bitch lets you pick yourself up and try again.

This chapter will discuss how positive thinking is the key to performance and why sports are so important for girls. But unlike previous chapters, there will be a lot of emphasis on The Bitch's—in this case, Sporty Bitch's—influence on boys and men. Why? Since many women date, marry, and raise male athletes, there are important things we need to know. Likewise, as women's sports become more important and competitive, this chapter will outline some male athletic pitfalls women need to avoid.

SPORTS PSYCHOLOGY: WHY THE MIND IS THE MOST IMPORTANT MUSCLE

Sports psychology began in the 1920s when some professors discovered that bicycle racers pumped faster if they were competing against groups of other cyclists. But the field wasn't very active until it burst forth in the 1970s with books about "inner" tennis and golf.

Suddenly everyone began talking about how the mind was the most important muscle in the body. Concentration exercises helped golfers repeat mantras of "back, hit" when they were swinging their club. Golfers who replaced their typical Bitchy chatter of "Oh, shit. Everyone is watching and I will probably miss the ball and make a complete ass of myself" with "back, hit" found their games magically improved.

Coaches who began using similar "inner tennis" methods found that players improved quickly. Even pros perfected their serves when they stopped negative self-talk like, "I can't hit a thing today" or "I'm doing so badly, I'll never win."

Previously, no one questioned the old adage, "Learn from your mistakes." So coaches in various sports taped games and edited everything out except the problems. But when they began doing the opposite—editing the tapes to only show great moves—performance soared. Athletes who could picture themselves succeeding, succeeded. Sports psychologists proved that athletes are like everyone else: we all tend to perform up—or down—to what we expect and see in our minds.

Every person who plays sports has probably experienced how Sporty Bitch made them lose. An excellent tennis player, Anna, remembered how a Bitchy reminder of humiliation made her lose a match she should have won easily.

"I was ranked the number one tennis player in high school," she told me, "but my first game in one tournament seeded me against a mean girl who had teased me in school. She was a much worse player than I was, but the thought of her harassment bothered me so much, I couldn't concentrate. She won! It was clearly my fault. I couldn't get over the mental hurdle and I blew it.

"In retrospect, I think a man might have used this to his advantage. Using his anger to spur his playing: imagining himself smashing the ball into her face and getting a lot of power from that."

Actually, I know lots of women who use aggression for power on the court—and lots of men who have more than equal opportunity problems with Sporty Bitch.

When I told an excellent weekend golfer about The Bitch, he said, "Sometimes I approach the ball and think, 'I bet I'm going to shank this into the woods,' and I do. But when I look at the green and visualize the ball going at the pin, it usually does. I should be able to remember this all the time, but I get blocked when things start going wrong. The Bitch takes over.

"Jack Nicklaus was the greatest golfer ever. I try to remember how obsessively positive he was. Once when he was asked what he didn't like about Augusta, he refused to answer. He didn't want any negative image in his mind."

SPORTS FOR GIRLS

In the 1960s and 1970s, when greater numbers of women began flooding into the workforce and climbing corporate ladders, experts began claiming that men had an unfair advantage because they played more team sports. What did boys learn from football and basketball that girls didn't learn from tennis? Team sports taught them to deal with competition and cooperation—to work as well with people you like as with people you don't.

The theory was that men who play basketball, for example, have to pass the ball to the best-positioned player, even if they can't stand the guy off court. And men who play football can bash and curse each other on the field, and then go out and order beers together afterward. This supposedly helped men avoid unproductive squabbling and politics at the office.

Other people felt that, in the age of equal opportunity, it was only fair to fund women's sports the same as men's. So, for many reasons, Title IX—part of the education amendments of 1972, which prohibited sex discrimination in public education and federally funded activities— was signed by Richard Nixon.

Ernestine Miller, a women's sports historian and writer, says, "Sports—especially team sports—do wonders to elate girls' self-esteem.

"Strong, toned, muscular bodies of female athletes are now considered glamorous and sexy. Women who care about physical conditioning have expanded our ideas of what is to be admired. That is extremely healthy for girls and women.

"The introduction of girls' team sports begins to teach important lessons early: cooperation and competition, how to lose and how to win. You learn to play your heart out and cope with enormous disappointments. The greatest lesson is how to lose, pick yourself up, and then come back and win."

A high school soccer coach cited another important lesson he had to teach many of his girls: to overcome The Bitch who doesn't let you see the difference between being selfish and having self-interest. "Girls are great team players," the coach told me, "so some of them have to learn that you don't always have to give the ball to the star. If you can make the goal, go for it yourself. You can be a star, too."

SPORTS FOR BOYS

The influence of sports on boys is more complex. It's not unusual for high school boys' football teams to brawl after a highly contested game, bashing each other with fists and helmets. Have you ever heard of Sporty Bitch making that happen after a girls' soccer game?

At the same time, if handled properly, athletics can give boys a healthy outlet for all their teenage aggression. And in poor neighborhoods where there are not enough positive male role models, coaches can become father figures, teaching boys to respect themselves and women, turning out athletes who are strong enough to be kind.

One such legendary coach, Mike Hawkins, worked at Germantown High School, on the Philadelphia border, with an almost entirely poor, black student body. Ten percent of the kids were homeless or in foster care, and one-third had special needs. Plus the school had a reputation for violence.

But Coach Hawkins did everything he could to give his students academic as well as athletic encouragement—the kind of support kids in wealthier districts experienced. He gave his players a word-of-the-day to memorize. He encouraged his players to be model citizens: to read to kids in a day care center and visit senior citizens at Christmas. He and his wife served dinner before each game, which was often the only sit-down meal the players ever had.

Then massive budget cuts hit the Philadelphia school system in 2013, forcing the closure of many schools and cutting the money for sports. Germantown High School was closed, and Coach Hawkins retired. The students were folded into their rival school, Martin Luther King. The question was: Could anyone keep up Coach Hawkins's positive influence on the boys, especially when they had to learn to play alongside their archrivals at King and had no money to pay coaches?

A filmmaker from Brooklyn, Judd Ehrlich, was so intrigued by this question that he made an award-winning documentary of the process, *We Could Be King* (2014). Anyone who watches it will cheer the new coach, Ed Dunn, a laid-off math teacher from Germantown who volunteers to be the head football coach. We watch as Dunn not only teaches the kids to play together and support each other, but how to become winners in life as well as on the field.

Judd Ehrlich told me, "Coaching is such a powerful way to fight against society's pressures. Many of these kids don't have dads, so Coach Dunn, who brings his eighteen-month-old son onto the field, is a great influence. And there are eight other volunteer coaches who live near the school, helping kids not just with athletics, but with their homework and with their lives on weekends."

While The Bitch and the media often make us think the worst about neighborhoods like Northwest Philadelphia, Ehrlich says his movie shows "there are a lot of adults who care. People who work in the school system and those who volunteer. One of the coaches is a police officer who told me he does this so he can get to the kids before they do something and he has to lock them up."

We Could Be King is not just a classic story of kids overcoming tremendous odds and obstacles to win. It also shows how coaches and sports help kids overcome the negative influences of mean streets—The Bitch that makes poor kids feel inferior or believe that the only way to succeed is through crime or drugs. One boy gets arrested and another is a truant. But both come back to school and succeed because of their love of sports and the positive intervention of the coaches.

"Some kids are really excited about math and biology," says Ehrlich. "But the things that appeal to most kids are the extra-curriculars. But those are the first things to be cut from school budgets.

"The girl cheerleaders lost their coach but kept on going by themselves. Even with their mismatched uniforms, they were a concrete representation of school spirit.

"When the football team began winning, it gave the kids in the school and people in the neighborhood something to believe in, pride in their school, and hope for the future.

"These kids are getting athletic scholarships and that makes it possible for them to go to college. They aren't going to go on to the NFL or NBA, but they are able to be the first person in their family to go to college and that has a great ripple effect on the community."

The Bitch, like negative coaches, teaches athletes that losing makes you a loser. Great coaches counter The Bitch by only using constructive criticism. They foster the concept of personal best and living a well-rounded life.

But there are far too many high schools and colleges where athletes can hardly write a sentence much less an academic essay. Schools that ignore kids' academic needs—or look the other way when athletes go on drunken rampages or rape co-eds—teach that success on the playing field is everything. But when the adulation stops, as it always does, Sporty Bitch is waiting to tell athletes they are nothing without the applause. And nothing is what they have to fall back on if they have gone to one of the schools where they have been treated more like gladiators than students.

WINNING IS EVERYTHING—LIFE WITH THE PROS

The scandals about concussions in boxing and football, and the doping scandals in baseball and bicycle racing, are proof that many athletes listen when Sporty Bitch says, "Winning is everything," or "Everybody's using drugs," or when she pushes "no pain, no gain" well beyond healthy limits. Essentially, Sporty Bitch says if you don't win, you are a loser. So do anything to win.

The pleasure of feeling your body exquisitely toned and achieving greater and greater results also comes with the pain of having to devote most of your life to training. It's hard to achieve balance when your Bitch is always pushing you to do one more push-up, one more lap.

As one swimmer said, after she stopped being an Olympic hopeful at age twenty-one, "I've never really done anything special for my birthday because I always had swimming practice or I was at a meet." After celebrating for the first time, she said, "I thought about just how fun it was to be a normal person."

If you have a Sporty Bitch in your head, even stunning successes and achievements don't bring happiness. NBA legend Jerry West explained in his book *West by West* that his losses live more in his memory than his successes. For example, he still hates to go to Boston because it reminds him of the times his Lakers lost to the Celtics in the 1960s. And he still denounces the "injustice" of not being named to an all-state basketball team when he was a boy.

"You need to possess more than a little nastiness to play basketball at the highest levels," he says. But it seems like the nastiest person around is his Sporty Bitch.

I'D RATHER DIE THAN STOP, BECAUSE WINNING IS EVERYTHING

When swimmers raise money for charities like Swim across America, a friend of mine, Lee Goldsmith, accompanies them as they try to swim around Manhattan or across Long Island Sound. Most of the swimmers are athletes who know their capacities, but sometimes he encounters swimmers who want to go farther and longer than is safe.

"If you are dealing with the last swimmers, they can get overtired or the tide will change and it can get dangerous," he told me. "Sometimes I have to stop them when they haven't achieved their goal.

"The women will understand that they are in danger. They will say, 'At least I tried. I did my best.' But the men often get an attitude. Even if they are clearly ill or exhausted, they say, 'I want to do more.' I have to force them out of the water.

"It's a self-image thing with men," he told me. "Women are engaged in the activity, but it's not their full identity. All too often, it is with men."

A woman at a yacht club told me a similar story. "I frostbite—race small boats in the winter. When there's a high wind, there's a danger of flipping over. In situations like that, men become much more aggressive than women. Even if it weren't dangerous to capsize in freezing water, you lose time if you capsize.

"Women are more interested in self-preservation. They think, 'Who's going to take care of the kids if I die out here?' It just isn't worth the risk."

But she worries that as women become more aggressive about winning, they will become more like men, and their Sporty Bitches will tell them that if they don't complete a race, much less win, they are a failure. So, more women will start to risk everything, too.

MID-LIFE CRISES

A psychologist I know said that she didn't care who her daughter married as long as he wasn't a major athlete. "I've seen too many very athletic men have terrible mid-life crises," she said.

I've seen that, too. Male athletes, like beautiful women, are especially vulnerable to mid-life crises because they have always counted on their bodies to give them success and admiration. The Bitch makes them think this will never end, and tells them they are "nothing" when it inevitably does.

Why is this predominantly a male problem? For one thing, female athletes don't usually get the fawning admiration that male athletes do. There may be some men and women hanging around outside the girls' locker room, dying to sleep with the star soccer goalie, but it's nothing like the groupies who idolize football heroes.

Also, athleticism is not part of what constitutes our image of femininity as it is for masculinity. When athletes begin to lose their strength and agility, it feels like they are losing their masculinity, too. Their Bitch says, "A real man can press his weight . . . You're over the hill! . . . Your pecs are as droopy as an old lady's boobs . . . No woman wants a man who isn't really strong."

For athletes, a loss of muscle tone often means a loss of machismo. And women who listened to Sporty Bitch when she said that the most important quality in a mate is athleticism are left holding an empty trophy, especially if Sporty Bitch tells their aging athletic mate that a fast car and a young girlfriend will make him feel like "a real man" again.

ANOTHER REASON WHY MEN ARE MORE VULNERABLE TO SPORTY BITCH

Why do men actually buy into the lie that winning is the only thing? Why do they push themselves to risk their lives when the only prize is bragging rights at an insignificant winter weekend sailing race? I can see a cartoon where a sheepish man says, "Testosterone made me do it." But Sporty Bitch has more on her side than hormones.

Just as the media pushes women to aspire to impossible standards of beauty, the media pushes men to achieve impossible standards of strength and courage. As one man told me, "My father grew up watching cowboy movies where John Wayne or Jimmy Stewart went out to face a gang of outlaws alone. They always won against all odds.

"I grew up with Spider-Man and Batman who did the same thing—and Rambo and all the others like him. Somehow it sinks into men that if they act strong and brave, they can't lose.

"So when a man is faced with a challenge, if he thought he would die, he would stop. But he knows other people have done it, so he thinks, 'I can do it, too. I'm not supposed to be afraid.'"

And there's a deeper, more hardwired instinct that lets the media messages soak in: researchers recently found that while the fight or flight instinct was thought to be universal, it's male, not female.

When faced with danger, psychologists always assumed that both men and women obeyed an instinct to take on the danger or run away as fast as possible. And we all know which choice movie heroes make: they never take flight if there is a fight.

But the American Psychological Association published research a decade ago that says women react in a different way to danger. Women "tend and befriend," instead of "fight or flight." Women tend to the kids—gather them and make sure they are in a safe place—and befriend other people who will help keep them and the kids secure.

Instinct tells women not to put their children in danger: Herd the kids and the old folks into the cave. Wait awhile and maybe the saber-toothed tiger will just go away. But what happens if the saber-toothed tiger attacks? Women can act like the fiercest, bravest mother lions if necessary—but only if necessary.

BANISHING THE BITCH

As this chapter shows, in sports, the mind is the most important muscle, and The Bitch can turn your mind against you. Sporty Bitch not only helps athletes talk themselves into poor performances, but makes them feel like failures if they don't win.

Here are some important ways to protect yourself, your family, and your community against The Bitch, so you can reap the benefits while avoiding the pitfalls of sports.

Work to make the way most women approach sports—that winning isn't everything—universally accepted. It's hard not to laugh when Jerry Seinfeld jokes that coming in second or winning the silver medal at the Olympics is like being told, "You're the number one loser," and "Of all the losers, you came in first." But jokes like that reinforce Sporty Bitch when she urges athletes to risk their health or their life in pursuit of a "win." Instead, support coaches and athletes who live by the words of the great sportswriter Grantland Rice, who wrote that it's "not that you won or lost, but how you played the game."

Support the concept of "personal best" instead of "winning is everything." Make sure that you and your family are participating in sports for the love of the game, for the great feeling of having an athletic, healthy body, and for the lessons learned in losing as well as winning.

Of course it's fun to cheer for the winners. But as every coach knows, it's much more difficult to do your best for the losing team than the winning one. The people who really try for their team even when there is little chance of winning are the real heroes.

Make sure the person who coaches you, your team, or your child is not the snarling kind of coach who creates a Bitch in people's heads. Support coaches who create men and women who are wise enough to care about academics as well as athletics and who are strong enough to be kind.

San Francisco reached out to high school coaches as part of its extremely successful effort to lower domestic violence. They taught the important message that real men do not hit women and children.

We all need to thank coaches who teach healthy values to our boys and girls. And to support their efforts with contributions if athletic budgets are cut. *We Could Be King* has attracted thousands of dollars in contributions to Martin Luther King High School in Philadelphia, but there are thousands of other struggling schools that need our help.

9

THE BLAME BITCH

Mistakes, Failure, and Inequity

People sometimes ask: Isn't The Bitch a good thing, like a conscience? No. Here's the difference: The Bitch encourages you to be insulting and cruel to yourself and others, while a conscience tries to keep you from acting that way. And if you have done something wrong, The Bitch wants you to wallow in guilt and shame, while a healthy conscience urges you to clear things up by apologizing and making amends.

So this chapter explores those issues by asking: What if you did something so stupid or bad that you harmed yourself and other people as well? Or what if you were unfairly harmed? Hmmm. Makes me think of my family.

My grandparents, Lyford and Dorothy Hornor, lived in a small Southern town, probably the only place in the world where, for several generations, if you were a Hornor, you were top dog. My grandfather owned the bank. They lived in one of the largest houses in town, a mansion complete with tall white columns.

Like many people with too much money and too little altruism, my grandfather self-destructed. He gambled, drank too much, and had affairs. He was well on the way to destroying his family when his mismanagement destroyed the bank.

After his failure, instead of depressing himself with Bitchy thoughts like, "Shame on you! You've ruined your life forever," in disgrace and relative poverty, he moved his family to Washington, D.C., where he found a job with the Federal Trade Commission and began leading an upright life, working hard for the first time in his life.

Bitchy shame would have been self-destructive, robbing my grandfather of the energy he needed to start over. Instead, he acknowledged his failings in a way that inspired him to learn from them and live in the opposite manner. He focused on behaving in a way that could win back his family's respect, rather than merely letting The Bitch beat him up.

As hard as it was for my grandfather to reconstruct his life, I think my grandmother's job was even more difficult. The Bitch flooded her with anger and resentment: her husband's stupid self-indulgence had harmed many people and left her friendless in a small one-bedroom apartment in a new city where she was a nobody, forever removed from the town and lifestyle she loved.

Like many people, my grandmother tried to find salvation through religion. And while she became very active at the National Cathedral, she was miserable until a popular book, *The Power of Positive Thinking*, helped her focus on building a good life for herself rather than wasting her energy resenting her husband and letting The Bitch tell her she was stupid and weak to stick by her mate.

By the time I came along, they had transformed themselves into a relatively happy old couple. He was a jolly grandpa who took me to the movies each Saturday and bought me popcorn. She taught me to cook the wonderful French-influenced Southern food she served to her new friends—people she knew who liked her for herself, not her money.

When the bank failed, my father lost the secure, indulged life of his childhood just as he was going to college. He told me that most weekends he lay in his bunk bed at The Citadel in Charleston, listening as music and laughter floated across the campus from parties where classmates were having fun. But he was too poor to attend.

All too often, The Bitch makes unlucky people like my father wallow in "why me?" thoughts. And she tells the poor that they are inferior, unworthy to enjoy what "their betters" have. But instead of indulging in these self-destructive thoughts, on those lonely school nights, my father focused on the future, promising himself that he would find a way to do well, do some good in the world, and create a positive life for himself and his family. And he did.

In a classic American success story, he invented a product and started manufacturing it in a garage, with my mom and me helping him box his product each night. As his business grew, he became one of the first equal opportunity employers in Baltimore, hiring men and women from every ethnic background, disabled and not.

Bitterness would have blocked the creativity he needed to succeed. If he had listened when his Bitch tried to tell him the world (or his father) had cheated him, it would have made him want to exploit his workers. Instead, he was an old-fashioned paternalist who helped his employees with all their personal problems. He paid for divorces from abusive spouses, and on weekend nights he occasionally bailed out someone who'd gone on a bender. His employees repaid him with the kind of loyalty rarely seen in companies these days.

MISTAKES ON THE JOB

When someone makes a mistake on the job, The Work Bitch advises a series of unproductive approaches that are more toxic to a career than the mistake itself. I discovered this years ago when I was writing my book *Divorcing a Corporation: How to Know When—and if—a Job Change Is Right for You* and came across a fascinating study on this topic.

The researchers were looking at what makes a successful career. Their starting assumption was that some people are just golden, with lucky streak careers that propel them straight up the ladder of success. But to test this theory, they interviewed twenty-one top executives and twenty managers whose careers got derailed.

Much to their surprise, the researchers found that all the executives were astonishingly alike: All forty-one were strong people who had at least one weakness that caused career setbacks. Every executive had faced serious management problems that had to be overcome, such as:

1. insensitivity to others, using a bullying, intimidating manner
2. a cool, aloof, and arrogant style
3. betrayal of trust, either by one-upmanship tactics or not following through on a promise
4. over-ambition
5. over-management of their people
6. inefficient staffing of their departments
7. the inability to adapt to a boss with a different style
8. too much dependency on a mentor
9. an inability to think strategically
10. weak results that created lower profits and lost accounts

No one was pure gold, so the question became how the successful group overcame their problems. The derailed executives exhibited a host of unproductive responses. They became defensive and rigid, denying their problems. They tried to shout down or ignore the negative feedback. Like Sporty Bitch, The Work Bitch often tells people that admitting a mistake or experiencing a failure makes them a loser.

But the executives who became CEOs didn't listen to that Bitchy advice. Instead, they showed a flexible, nondefensive attitude when faced with a setback. They used their energy to admit and correct, rather than deny, their problems.

Managers tell me that a mistake or missed deadline will usually not derail a career these days unless the employee tries to hide the mistake or doesn't give advance warning that the deadline will not be met. When The Bitch advises employees to ignore or cover up problems, it rarely works. Managers hate it when something unexpected blows up.

An executive consultant told me, "If you're any good, you're going to take risks, and that means you're going to have many successes and some failures. Meet your failures head-on. In most cases, the people you failed will appreciate your candor and you'll keep their support." So, if you make a mistake, even a big one, The Bitch may try to tell you that you would look weak or stupid to admit it. But the best strategy is usually the opposite: own up to it, pledge to correct it, and vow to learn lessons from it, so it will never happen again.

So if your Bitch is telling you that only losers make mistakes, or that you will never be forgiven, or that your boss will think you are stupid if she finds out what you did, think again. If you really did something stupid, you will probably seem smarter if you tell the boss, "I did something very stupid. I'm sorry and this is how I would like to correct it so it will never happen again."

MISTAKES WITHIN THE FAMILY

What if you did something mean to your child? Perhaps you called her an insulting name or you slapped him. If your Bitch says you would look weak if you apologized to your child, think again. What kind of example are you setting? What kind of person do you want your child to grow up to be?

If you want your child to be the kind of person who has good relationships with other people, begin by setting a good example by being someone strong enough to admit when they are wrong, someone secure enough to say "I'm sorry."

If you grew up in a home where an apology was met with "Sorry isn't enough," you want to be different. If you grew up in a home where blame had to be apportioned and someone always had to be the "bad" one, your Bitch will probably tell you that an apology will just make you "it." But in happy households, an apology usually clears the air and clears the blame.

When children apologize for doing something wrong, it doesn't necessarily mean that all is forgiven. If a serious rule was broken, there may have to be consequences or some restitution. But an apology is the first step in clearing the air and restoring the relationship of trust, so the process of resolving the problem may begin.

MARITAL MISTAKES: INFIDELITY

When the whole PMS (Premenstrual Syndrome) conflict was raging—with some people claiming it was a reason why women should not be leaders—several of my colleagues decided to propose an equally hormonal problem that affects some men, making them equally unfit to lead. Their proposed diagnosis was TTS, Testicular Tension Syndrome, for men who cannot keep their trousers zipped.

But just because we all laughed at TTS it didn't mean that as therapists we thought infidelity was funny, or that we didn't know it has become almost as common with women as men. No matter who does it or why, it usually causes a great deal of pain.

Even so, I have worked with many, many couples whose marriages not only survived, but were even strengthened after an affair. And I have found there are three requirements to save a marriage after infidelity:

1. The unfaithful partner has to express genuine remorse.
2. The affair must be ended.
3. There has to be a genuine intent and promise to be faithful in the future.

The Bitch may try to advise a cheating spouse, "Lay low and try again." She may make an unfaithful partner believe their spouse will never truly love him or her again, and so it doesn't matter. But with infidelity, it's usually two strikes and you're out.

On the other hand, the "innocent" spouse cannot fall prey to The Bitch when she tries to evoke unhealthy reactions like:

1. "I will never forgive you!" A cheating spouse who makes a contrite apology, promises to end the affair, and never have another one usually deserves a second chance. One apology may not be enough, but demands for apologies to be repeated over and over are unreasonable. The couple must jointly decide when the apologies can stop.

2. "I will never trust you again!" Trust has to be rebuilt. The person who had the affair should be willing to take active steps to prove himself or herself trustworthy, like allowing the spouse to look at all cell phones, landline records, and credit card bills to verify honesty. And, again, the couple must jointly decide when it is reasonable for this scrutiny to stop.

3. "It was all your fault!" Well, of course the person who committed adultery must shoulder most of the blame, but rather than indulging in an unproductive Blame Game—always a Bitch favorite sport!—a non-judgmental examination of the marriage will usually reveal unhappiness that led one partner to seek gratification elsewhere. Even if the root cause lies in a mid-life crisis or simply succumbing to overwhelming temptation, an examination of how to make the marriage happier on both sides will create stronger bonds.

ADDICTIONS AND AMENDS

Anyone who makes a mistake is tempted to deny it. But if every day is chock full of mistakes, then denial becomes a way of life. That's what happens with alcoholics and drug addicts: denial is the only way they can maintain their addiction and the destruction it causes.

A therapist I'll call Barbara, because she wants to remain anonymous, treats drug and alcohol problems. A recovering alcoholic herself, she explained to me, "Alcoholics become sneaky. They have to hide what they are doing. They will tell you anything to get you off their back—'Oh, I'm sorry' . . . 'I'll get right on that'—but they will do nothing because they want to put their energy toward drinking and drugging.

"They will argue with their spouse all the time because they want someone or something to blame for their behavior. They want to be able to say, 'If you were in my marriage, you'd drink, too.' Or 'I have this terrible back pain, so I have to take these pills' or 'I drink because my life has been so sad.'

"Most people with drug and alcohol problems are using chemicals to manage their emotions. Maybe they grew up with very critical parents and are very self-critical to themselves. They drink to try to drown out their inner voice that you are calling The Bitch.

"Maybe they never learned to control their anger and after a few drinks they let it out, ranting and raging. They may think that if they stop drinking, everything will be okay. But often they need to learn how to manage their emotions in a different way. AA [Alcoholics Anonymous] helps people do that."

Like many addiction counselors, Barbara was an alcoholic. For years, she maintained what looked like a normal life but got drunk every night. Like most alcoholics, her Bitch made her ashamed of "needing" alcohol, so she denied she had a problem for years. She didn't hit bottom, but she did hit the bottom of a flight of stairs.

As she says, "One night I went to a fortieth birthday party for a friend in the upstairs room of a fancy restaurant. I kept ordering Sambuca after dinner to a point where I fell down the stairs and blacked out.

"The next morning I had a horrible hangover and didn't remember a thing. When I heard what I had done, I realized I couldn't keep living this way anymore. I felt too sick to do anything for two days, but then I found a beginner's AA meeting and never had another drink.

"At first, you are often too ashamed to admit the harm you have done to other people. You are very self-involved with internal voices that tell you, 'you're no good' . . . 'you'll never stop drinking' . . . 'you're a mess' . . . 'nobody loves you.'"

These mean voices in your head—The Bitch—are called "The Committee" by AA members. And Barbara says, "People at AA meetings help you counter 'The Committee.'

"Eventually you get to a point where you realize if you want to increase your self-esteem, you have to behave in ways that make you proud of yourself. You may have done a lot of wrong things, but you see that you have the opportunity to do the next right thing.

"As you work your way through the twelve-step program with the help of your sponsor and everyone else at meetings, you get to a point where you feel strong enough to reach Step 8: Make a list of all the people you have harmed and become willing to make amends to them. Then Step 9 is actually making those amends.

"I went to my employer and apologized for all the sick days I cheated him out of because I was hung-over. I apologized to my husband for the nights I stole from him when I was drunk and not really with him, or when I embarrassed him. I apologized to my son for sometimes showing up drunk to take him home from school and because he couldn't bring friends home since he never knew what condition I was going to be in."

Barbara says that most addicts, like everyone else, are terrified of apologizing. But she says, "Just standing up and taking responsibility makes you one step closer to being restored. When you apologize to another person, you are setting up a different and healthier relationship. Saying 'I was wrong' is a real turning point for change and making amends.

"Sometimes, like in my case, just living a good life in the future is all the restitution that is necessary."

Even though it has been fifteen years since Barbara had her last drink, she still attends AA meetings regularly because she still has the urge to drink sometimes. "I can go to any city or decent-sized town and find a meeting. I've gone to meetings in cities from Nantucket to Memphis and been welcomed. It's like belonging to a sorority," a sorority dedicated to countering The Bitch who says, "One drink won't matter" or "You are just no good."

CRIME: RECONCILIATION AND RESTITUTION

The idea of making amends, so key to Alcoholics Anonymous, is gaining ground in criminal justice systems around the world. In the United

States, at least one-third of all states now require judges to consider having the perpetrator make restitution to the victim.

For example, a thief who stole a television would have to replace it, perhaps in lieu of going to jail. A drunk driver who wrecked someone's car would pay to have the car restored and also clear any medical bills related to the crash. A rapist would pay for the victim's therapy.

While restitution grew out of the victim's rights movement, it can be as healing to the perpetrator as the victim, giving the criminal a way to atone for the crime and offering a healthy outlet for remorse and shame. The most dramatic examples of this are probably seen in Rwanda where, twenty years after Hutus and Tutsis mercilessly killed almost a million of each other, there is a formal program that encourages and facilitates reconciliation.

It starts when the perpetrator, usually a male Hutu, requests pardon from his victim, usually a female Tutsi, who may have been raped or mutilated when her family was killed. The perpetrator may have "paid" for his crime by going to jail, but as one said, "My conscience was not quiet," so he applied to the program, formally requesting forgiveness from his victim. If the victim accepts the request, a meeting and some form of restitution is made.

Sometimes the restitution is symbolic, such as giving a basket of food. Other times it is an offer to support and protect the woman who was made a widow, or to rebuild the house that he destroyed.

Victims report that sometimes the most valuable thing they receive through the program is not the financial reward, but the sense of calm they feel after forgiving and dropping the corrosive hate they lived with for twenty years.

BANISHING THE BITCH

If you have done something wrong, The Bitch may tell you there is no way to assuage your guilt. She may say that offering an apology will make you look weak and open you up to criticism or abuse. But offering an apology and trying to make amends is your first step in leading a guilt-free life. Whether the person accepts your apology or not, you know that you have done the right thing.

Stop wallowing in guilt. That doesn't help anyone. Torturing yourself with endless thoughts like, "You're a terrible person!" or "You don't deserve to be forgiven" is merely self-indulgent. If you are really sorry about something you did, find a way to make an apology. If that apology would do more damage than good (as in the case of revealing an affair to an unsuspecting spouse), find a way to clear your conscience without inflicting pain on another person.

Confront denial. If your Bitch is whispering, "They're making a big deal about nothing," you are probably in denial. And denial usually makes the problem bigger. There is usually nothing more annoying to a person who deserves a genuine apology than to have you deny or try to excuse your bad behavior. Often an honest apology can help heal the wounds you created, no matter what they are. You might not be forgiven, but at least you have tried to take ownership of the problem and make amends.

Regain your pride. If you want to be proud of yourself, do something that makes you proud. That can start with admitting your mistakes and making amends to the person you hurt—including yourself. Learn from your mistakes and live a life that gives you healthy pleasure and pride. And don't ever let The Bitch say you don't deserve that. You can't go back and change the wrong things you did. But you can try to do the right thing from now on.

10

THE BITCH AT NIGHT

Sleep Tight, Don't Let The Bitch Bite

Some people are so busy and distracted during the day that The Bitch can't intrude on their thoughts. But there she is, loud and clear at 2:00 or 3:00 a.m., torturing people with insomnia all night long.

Ann Leary wrote a wonderful description of Bitch-fueled insomnia in her novel *The Good House*. As the main character, Hildy Good complains, "I have no trouble falling asleep, especially after concluding an evening with a little wine, but I tend to awaken with a start at exactly three a.m. filled with dread and self-loathing. It's my own little hell, where I'm visited by a cast of demons who delight in reminding me of my daily wretchedness, my lifelong wickedness. An inventory of the previous day's mishaps is reviewed, followed by the unscrolling of a decades-long catalog of my own sins, spites, regrets, and grudges."

The Bitch plagues other insomniacs with middle-of-the-night fears like: "How will I pay the bills?" or "How will I ever find a job . . . love . . . success . . . or the way to the airport?" And, of course, there are the ever-popular angry midnight tirades: "How could my boss, parent, friend, or lover be so unfair, rude, or mean?"

As you thrash around with upsetting thoughts running through your mind, you can be sure The Bitch will also make you obsessively watch the clock, agonizing, "It's three o'clock! I'll never get back to sleep! I'll be exhausted at work tomorrow!"

I don't have to explain insomnia. Anyone who has it by now is thinking, "Yeah, yeah, I know what it is. How do I get rid of it?"

The first and most important fact to know is what The Bitch and the pharmaceutical industry want to keep secret: The worry and frustration over your lack of sleep is more exhausting than the lack of sleep itself. In fact, lying quietly while meditating or relaxing is almost as healthy as sleeping. So if you wake up and just relax instead of spending the rest of the night tossing, turning, worrying, and fretting, you will feel almost as rested and healthy as if you had been asleep.

Here's another important fact about insomnia: psychoanalytic, behavioral, and cognitive psychologists each have effective techniques to banish The Bitch at night. So while The Bitch might be encouraging you to use sleeping pills, which can be addictive and even make your sleep problems worse, try one of these psychological cures first. By the time you finish this chapter, you will be able to choose the one that's right for you.

THE PSYCHOANALYTIC APPROACH

Everyone knows that fears and worries are almost always exaggerated when you wake up in the middle of the night. Concerns that seem horrible at 3:00 a.m. can often be dismissed the next morning. Sometimes, however, the issues that wake you are symptoms or symbols of real problems that need to be addressed. But The Bitch likes to keep the real issues hidden, so her nightly torment can continue.

For example, Ann Leary's character, Hildy Good, doesn't just have "a little wine" each night; she's an alcoholic. But Hildy, like most alcoholics, is in denial. Also, like others who drink too much, she has no problem falling asleep, but awakens in the middle of the night. Hildy's past transgressions are real and, like her insomnia, caused by her drinking. Once she stops denying her alcoholism and stops drinking, she also stops behaving badly and begins to sleep through the night.

So try to be honest with yourself to see if the reasons for your wakefulness become clear. If not, is there any symbolic meaning to them? For example, if you always wake up at two o'clock, did anything happen to you at two o'clock in the past? Or are you concerned about a relationship—the "two" of you?

The Bitch at night doesn't always torture people with words. Sometimes she uses symbolic, disturbing dreams. So if you are awakened by a recurring dream, consider if there is a hidden meaning like this: I once had a patient who kept dreaming about a deer with huge antlers waiting for her in a parking lot after work each night. It turns out she was missing a dear, not a deer, who used to meet her commuter train and drive her home. Once she began working on the issues surrounding the loss of her "dear," her insomnia disappeared.

If you feel your dreams are symbolic but can't figure them out, a psychologist can help unravel the meaning behind your nightly upset. Here's an example:

Deborah is an architect in Connecticut, who specializes in renovating and redecorating dentists' offices. She does her work so beautifully, so efficiently, and so cost effectively that each client usually recommends her to another. So Deborah works not just in neighboring towns, but in Rhode Island and New York as well.

With a successful practice, a loving marriage, and two cute kids, Deborah was a happy woman until, in her mid-thirties, she began waking up at night obsessed with a terrifying image: She was dead and eternally floating alone in cold, dark outer space. She could see stars, planets, and galaxies, but never any human beings.

Deborah had never been afraid to die. So when she started waking up shaking with fear, she tried to comfort herself, saying that if there's no Heaven, death is undoubtedly just eternal sleep, not utter loneliness in outer space. But logic and rational thinking didn't help. And nothing—not a thick duvet nor snuggles with her sleepy husband—could shake The Bitch's chilly, deathly image of being absolutely alone. Tossing and turning half the night several times a week, she became so upset that she consulted me about the problem.

Paradoxically, people who fear death are usually the ones who feel they are not "really living" because something important is missing in their lives. When that hole is filled and life becomes more fulfilling, their fear of death diminishes. So I wondered if something was missing in Deborah's life. Her dream was about being alone, but how could she feel lonely when her life was so full of work and family?

In the middle of a conversation about loneliness, Deborah remembered a cartoon she had seen, where a busy, middle-aged woman said, "Whoops, I forgot to have children!" If she were in that cartoon, Deborah said she would be saying, "Whoops, I forgot to have friends!"

Deborah was an only child who grew up in a small town in Ohio. Her aging parents and childhood friends still lived there. When she went to college in Maryland, she made friends but didn't keep up with them when she moved to Philadelphia, because all her time was taken up with rigorous graduate classes and her relationship with the man she eventually married. When her husband's job took them to Connecticut, she hoped to make close friendships with some of her colleagues, but she was the youngest person and only woman in a small architectural firm, so nothing jelled before she began working on her own.

A husband, children, and good job would be more than enough for many women, but Deborah realized how very much she missed having the support and intimacy of female friendships.

"If something happened to my husband, I would be completely alone," she told me. "If I got sick, I don't think anyone would visit me in the hospital or offer to take care of my kids. My husband and I occasionally go to dinner with other couples, but I don't know any of the wives well enough to even ask them out for a girls' lunch."

Deborah quickly realized that she wanted more than just a friend or two. She longed to be part of a circle of friends, to feel the support of a community. Someone else with similar needs might join a club or professional group, but Deborah, with typical entrepreneurial energy, started a neighborhood association that met on a monthly basis and a mother-daughter book club with her pre-teen child. She also joined a Bible-study group at her church.

Most of her new activities were crammed into nights and weekends, but she cut back a little on her work hours so she could ask at least one new friend a week to have lunch.

Deborah obviously didn't become close friends with everyone she met. After six months, she dropped out of the study group at church, and when her daughter entered high school, the book group ended. But by then Deborah had made some good friends and felt part of a supportive community in her neighborhood, church, and local school system.

Shortly after she defined her problem and went to work solving it, she began to sleep better. The Bitch could no longer torment her with thoughts and dreams that she was friendless and alone.

THE BEHAVIORAL APPROACH

You'll never get back to sleep. And if you do, you'll just wake up again soon. You will always have insomnia—and it will kill you! Regardless of what The Bitch is saying to make you to toss and turn, behavioral psychologists believe the key to a good night's sleep is healthy bedtime behavior.

Behavioral Bedtime Rule #1: Follow a Routine

Establish a calming pre-sleep routine that quiets your mind and body. Most adults, like children, sleep better if they go to bed at the same time each night after a relaxing ritual that lets them wind down.

For instance, parents who let their children run around until they are tired are making a huge mistake. Kids (and adults) get crabby and strung out, not sleepy, if before-bed activities are too stimulating. A warm bath, followed by quiet music and a calming book before lights-out, is what children, and many adults, need.

Something that interferes with our healthy routine, like jet lag, can give The Bitch an opportunity to torture us. That's what happened to Kathy. Kathy is a baker. Short and jolly, she could live on cake. For her fiftieth birthday, her husband fulfilled her lifelong dream by enrolling her in a cooking course in Paris.

For two weeks in France, Kathy woke up at seven every morning excited about learning the secrets of making flaky croissants, golden brioche, and tiny raspberry tarts. She went to sleep each night, promptly at ten, dreaming about glazes, custard fillings, and rolling pins. Jet lag was no problem at all, until she returned home to Chicago.

Kathy's happy habit of rising at 7:00 a.m. Paris time meant that she was wide awake at midnight in Chicago. And her French bedtime meant she was yawning at three in the afternoon. Since Kathy's husband didn't like coming home after work to find her napping, she forced herself to stay up until after dinner. But as soon as dessert was finished, The Bitch whispered, "You're so tired, why don't you just go to bed?"

Kathy was snoring by eight each night. Waking at midnight, she would toss and turn for hours, with The Bitch admonishing, "Four hours is not enough sleep!" . . . "You will be exhausted tomorrow morning!" . . . "The bags under your eyes are getting worse and worse!"

Who could sleep with that racket in their head? After fitfully dozing, she would finally get out of bed at 4:00 a.m. and bake something delicious for breakfast.

Kathy was a homemaker, so she didn't have to worry about getting to work, but she did have to worry about the extra pounds she and her husband were gaining from devouring hot, buttered breakfast rolls every morning. She also missed spending evenings with her husband, watching their favorite TV shows and going to concerts. When her husband invited an attractive single neighbor to use her ticket to the symphony, Kathy was afraid she was going to lose her husband as well as her health. So, even though The Bitch said she would never sleep well again, Kathy began a behavioral approach that solved her problems.

While Kathy's sleep schedule changed all at once after being in a different time zone, behavioral psychologists have found that reestablishing a normal bedtime has to be a gradual process: pushing back bedtime a little each night and getting out of bed a little later each morning.

Realizing that a big dinner made her feel logy, Kathy began having a light supper, and instead of letting The Bitch rush her off to bed, she forced herself to take a nightly walk around her neighborhood. If the weather was bad, she went to the gym for an hour. She thought exercise would make her more tired, but it was stimulating and enabled her to stay up longer.

When Kathy woke up early, instead of saying, for example, "Oh, my God, I'll never get back to sleep," she told herself, "I'll just lie here and relax a little while longer." Slowly, with exercise, a change in eating, and reassuring thoughts when she woke up too early, Kathy readjusted her inner time clock. Now, although her husband misses waking up to the smell of fresh-baked bread, Kathy is very happy to be back sleeping well on Chicago time.

Behavioral Bedtime Rule #2: If You Can't Sleep, Get out of Bed

Your bed should only be used for sleeping. Yes, of course, sex in bed is fine, but the point is, when you wake up in the middle of the night, behaviorists say you should never use the bed for worrying and thrashing. So, if you wake up, can't get back to sleep, and The Bitch starts tormenting you, get out of bed and do something calming or boring until you feel drowsy. Then come back to bed to sleep. Baking was too stimulating for Kathy, so instead when she woke up too early and couldn't get back to sleep with just relaxing thoughts, she caught up on her reading in another room until she felt sleepy and went back to bed again.

When my husband began waking up in the middle of the night, The Bitch began feeding him her usual routine: "You will never get back to sleep! You'll be exhausted tomorrow and won't be effective at work!" Predictably, these worries kept him awake, thrashing around so that, in fact, he did feel too tired to work as effectively as usual.

I had gone to a few sleep workshops and assured him that lying quietly in bed is almost as healthy as sleeping, but he didn't believe me. I also told him that behavioral psychologists advise clients to get up and do boring tasks like washing the floor or paying bills, thinking how nice it would be if I woke up and found that, as if by magic, my kitchen floor had been cleaned. But my husband dismissed all my expert advice. (We are never prophets in our own land.)

Then he read that in some "primitive" cultures there is something called "second sleep," which means that it's normal for people to go to sleep, then wake up and do something in the middle of the night before going back to sleep again. So instead of thrashing and worrying, he told his Bitch that waking was perfectly natural. But what should he get up and do?

While telling me about "second sleep" cultures, he mentioned that natives often wake their spouses and friends to chat or dance. I replied that while I would be very happy if he got up and washed the floors, waking me for a 2:00 a.m. tango would be legitimate grounds for divorce. And calling our neighbors for a starlit schmooze would be even worse.

Deprived of those options, when my husband wakes up and can't get back to sleep, he enjoys reading or listening to music for a while before going back for his "second sleep." But I'm still hoping that washing the floors will seem like a better option.

THE COGNITIVE APPROACH

Cognitive psychologists suggest that the key to a good night's sleep lies not so much in what you do, but in what you think. If you wake up in the middle of the night with a great idea and The Bitch says, "You'll never remember this in the morning," you will toss and turn, worried that you will forget. Or if—BOING!!—you open your eyes and find yourself wide awake at two, three, or four o'clock and you believe The Bitch when she says, "You'll never get back to sleep" or "Don't be a fool. Only sleep, not just relaxing or meditating, will make you feel well rested," that will probably be the case. This is called a self-fulfilling prophecy.

So here's the simplest solution to some sleep problems: Put a pad of paper and a pencil beside your bed. If you wake up in the middle of the night with a brilliant idea or a task for tomorrow that you don't want to forget, write it down and go back to sleep, knowing that it will be there for you to remember in the morning.

If you wake up worrying about something, write that down, too. Once it's on paper, tell yourself, "I'll worry about this tomorrow." This isn't a Scarlett O'Hara avoidance tactic. It's healthy and rational for several reasons.

First, middle-of-the-night worries almost always seem worse than they are. Second, it's very difficult to think effectively about solving problems late at night when your brain is muddled. Third, in the morning, it's not only easier to think clearly, but also sometimes your unconscious mind has been working overnight to come up with a solution. As John Steinbeck once wrote, "It's a common experience that a problem difficult at night is resolved in the morning after the committee of sleep has worked on it."

Several years ago, I started waking up at three every night, with nothing on my mind except how in the world to get back to a good night's sleep. When this continued night after night, I went through the sequence of possibilities described in this chapter.

First, I checked the psychoanalytic approach, asking myself: Is there anything symbolic about three o'clock? No. Is there anything symbolic about what I was worrying about? No. It was just the ordinary Bitch routine: "Oh, my God, it's three in the morning, and you'll never get back to sleep. You have to get up at seven, and you'll probably be so tired that you will fall asleep in one of your sessions."

So, I tried the behavioral approach. I didn't want to wash the floors or do my bills—that sounded just too unpleasant. But I liked the idea of getting up and reading a good book. Unfortunately, I found that for me, reading in the middle of the night was addictive. I began waking up just to get my reading done.

Thankfully, the cognitive approach worked for me. It involved calming my mind with positive mental images and calming my anxiety with what I learned in the sleep workshops: that just lying restfully or meditating is almost as healthy as sleep. Even though I knew this was true, my Bitch whispered, "You don't believe that crap, do you? You'll never be able to just lie there and relax. And even if you do, you will be exhausted the next morning!" But even though I was a skeptic, cognitive psychology outsmarted my Bitch!

To still my mind and meditate, I had to find an extremely pleasant, restful image to concentrate on. I came up with lying on the bow of a sailboat, dozing in the warmth of a summer day, soothed by gentle rocking waves, while someone else quietly steered the boat. Unlike real life, in this image, I never have to worry about getting sunburned or getting back to shore on time. I can feel delightfully warm and lazy.

So I put this image in my mind and told myself the anti-insomnia mantra: even if you don't get back to sleep, just lying peacefully, enjoying your image is almost as good as sleeping. This put me in a win–win situation: I could either rest or sleep, since both were good for me. And it worked!

So most nights, I sleep well. But if I awake and start tossing and turning, I invoke my sailboat image. If I start obsessively looking at the clock, instead of saying, "Oh, my God, it's four o'clock and I'm still awake!!!" I tell myself, "Oh, this is great. It's four o'clock and I still have three more hours to just meditate or sleep. Either one is fine."

My Bitch still tries to keep me awake with worries, but I tell her to shut up while I go to my mental sailboat. She is never allowed aboard. So within a few minutes of telling myself that I have hours to mentally lie in the sun, I am happily snoozing.

BANISHING THE BITCH

Many people experience their Bitch most forcefully in the middle of the night. It's easy to lose track of logic when you are tired. Worries loom larger in the dark than in the light of day. But this chapter has given you time-tested tools to get the rest—if not the sleep—you crave.

Pick the method that works for you. One of these methods should work best. If it stops working, reconfigure it or try another.

If none of these methods work, consider whether your problem is depression. In the rare case that none of these methods cures your insomnia, sleeplessness may be a symptom of depression. If you have other symptoms, such as a change in weight, a feeling of lethargy making it difficult to do things like get out of bed and brush your teeth, or if you are feeling very sad, weepy, hopeless, or helpless, get yourself to a professional who can prescribe an antidepressant. An antidepressant treats the chemical imbalance that can cause depression and sleep problems.

Use sleep medications only as a last resource. In my opinion, sleep medication should only be used on a very short-term basis. The danger is that you will begin feeling like Alice in Wonderland, with The Bitch saying, "eat me" every night. A professional who deals with medication can help you if you feel you have become dependent on sleeping pills.

Whatever happens, just don't believe The Bitch when she tells you your sleep problem can never be solved.

11

THE PARTY BITCH
Never Invite Her

The Party Bitch has so many ways to kill the fun. When you open a beautiful invitation to a party at a place you would love to see, but don't know anyone else who will be going, The Bitch will tell you: "You won't know a soul. You'll just stand around looking stupid." And she'll say that if you try to talk to people, you won't know what to say, so they'll *know* you're stupid.

If you crank up your courage and attend, the next morning, as soon as your eyes pop open, there she'll be, waiting to rehash the "stupid" things you said and did. As a woman who lives in Washington State told me, "I pull the sheet over my head, saying, 'Ashamed!'"

And she's just as cruel to people who want to entertain. Consider inviting friends over and Party Bitch predicts you'll burn the food and the guests will be bored or boring. Even successful, confident people succumb to these disastrous predictions. An actress who is completely comfortable in front of huge audiences confessed, "I don't throw dinner parties. I'm generally too scared to fail."

And speaking of being afraid, it is amazing how The Bitch can make hosts afraid to confront terrible behavior by houseguests.

GOING TO A PARTY ALONE
IS FINE—IF YOU DON'T TAKE THE BITCH

Everyone, except an extreme extrovert, is uncomfortable going to a party alone and entering a room full of strangers. But for shy people, going to any party is difficult and going alone seems impossible.

The Bitch makes shy people imagine that everyone will be judging and observing them, watching for mistakes and laughing about them behind their backs. Here's why that's a lie: confident people will be too focused on having a good time to worry about you, and people lacking in self-confidence will be too self-absorbed, worried about their own discomfort and mistakes to focus on yours.

A young woman in her twenties consulted me because, among other things, she was afraid to attend parties by herself. She had moved to New York and didn't know many people. But she was in a job where she received many invitations to exciting events in beautiful venues. Even if she accepted an invitation, she was usually too shy to show up unless she could convince someone to go with her.

I told her a very Bitch-defeating truth: Never underestimate how insecure everyone is. She didn't believe me when I said that people standing by themselves looking haughty are usually just afraid no one will talk to them. So a good trick for overcoming social anxiety at a party is to go up to someone standing alone, or to a couple who are standing around looking awkward, and introduce yourself. They will usually be extremely relieved to have someone to talk to.

There was a battle in her mind: Should she believe me or her Bitch? Would other people who were alone welcome her? Or, as The Party Bitch told her, would they just give her a cold stare and either ignore her, or say, "What do *you* want?"

She decided she had nothing to lose by testing out my theory and found it worked like magic. Now she has no problem going to parties: she just walks up to other people who are by themselves, knowing they will be grateful that she has saved them from "social oblivion."

But what if your Bitch makes you afraid that once you introduce yourself, you won't know what to say? Here's the cynical truth she doesn't want you to know: most people would much rather talk about themselves than hear anything interesting you might have to say. So get comfortable asking a few leading questions.

For example, at a charity fundraiser, you could start with, "How are you connected with the organization?" Or at a private party, the most obvious opener is, "How do you know the hostess?" You can follow with conversational ploys like, "Where did you grow up?" or "What do you like to do when you're not working?" And if you are talking to a stay-at-home mom, you can ask, "What do you like to do when you aren't taking care of your kids?" The point is that if you get people talking about themselves, even if you don't say a word, they will think you are the best conversationalist they have met in a long time.

THE BITCH IS WAITING TO POUNCE THE NEXT MORNING

If you aren't afraid to go to parties (and instead love them a little too much), you know that sometimes one drink can lead to another, which, in turn, can hinder your judgment. When you open your eyes the next morning, your Bitch is waiting to tell you what a fool you made of yourself. You said the *stupidest* thing! Or you did the most *embarrassing* thing. *Everyone* is talking about it!

On college campuses, there is something called "the walk of shame" for women who had so much to drink that they got "beer goggles." You wake up the next morning in some strange bed next to someone you don't know and vaguely remember that this guy seemed cute at the frat party. The Party Bitch might have said, "Go for it!" but this morning she's saying, "What in the world were you thinking, you stupid slut?!"

What's done is done. Hold your head high and vow to put corrective lenses in your goggles from now on.

THE DINNER PARTY: VERSION #1

Carla is a sophisticated New York writer with a beautiful apartment on the Upper East Side of Manhattan. Real estate is so expensive in New York that most apartments only have a small dining area in the living room, but Carla has a large, formal dining room. Unfortunately, her Party Bitch, who demands perfection, makes Carla too nervous to use it.

Even family dinners when her adult kids come to visit are ordeals for Carla. She tries to make the Eastern European food her mother made—goulashes and stews with cinnamon-laced cakes for dessert. But when the Party Bitch criticizes her messy kitchen or her choice of meat, Carla becomes so agitated that she yells at anyone who comes into the kitchen. She gets so nervous reading recipes that she leaves out ingredients and gets the timing wrong. Guests sit in the living room, listening to Carla bang pots and curse. It's no fun for anyone.

"Even when I take a tranquilizer, I get nervous and worried," she told me. "I got into a bad habit of having a glass of wine or two while I'm cooking, but that makes me muddle-headed. I'm giving up!"

When not in the kitchen, Carla is friendly and gregarious. No one would ever guess that she's so insecure about entertaining. If friends wonder why they've never been to her home for anything more than a glass of wine and a few nuts, they probably just think Carla's too busy to cook.

THE DINNER PARTY: VERSION #2

Unlike most of her friends in Brooklyn, Reba loves to cook. On weekends, she spends happy hours poring over cookbooks, testing recipes, and planning dinner parties. Sounds Bitch-proof, doesn't it?

Reba works such long hours that she can barely squeeze in an hour at the gym before coming home and collapsing into bed. So, when she wakes up on Saturday morning expecting five or six people for dinner that night, she has to shop, clean, and prepare the meal before they arrive.

In the grocery store, Reba sees chickens she could easily roast, or salmon she could just throw under the broiler, but her Bitch says, "Oh, but Beef Bourguignon would be so much better." And when she is tempted to buy brownies for dessert, The Bitch advises, "You should bake from scratch. It won't take that much time, and they will taste much more delicious."

So Reba goes into whirlwind mode and gets everything done. She purees spinach for the vegetable terrine, melts chocolate for the brownies, and simmers beef, carrots, and mushrooms in red wine. It's all complex and delicious. She loves the work, even though beads of sweat trickle down her head, making her hair spring up into thick damp curls.

But by the time the guests arrive, Reba is exhausted. She drinks too much wine and wonders why she didn't have as much fun as she expected.

THE DINNER PARTY: VERSION #3

The Bitch tells you that a few more people won't make any difference. She chuckles and says, "The more the merrier," making you forget that more guests mean more work—not to mention that you don't have room for all those people.

Brenda was famous for giving the best parties in Baltimore. Everyone thought she entertained with ease. And she did, until The Bitch encouraged her to let things get way out of control. Here is what Brenda told me:

"Our first New Year's Eve party was at our new house. We only had one piece of furniture in the living room and the walls needed to be painted, but we invited a few friends over and hung crepe paper streamers to make it look like a prom in a high school gym. It was pot luck, so everyone brought a dish. It couldn't be anything but relaxed because of the ambience. It started a tradition.

"The next year the guest list had grown to fourteen. We had a sit-down dinner and everyone brought something. Everyone had such a good time that more of our friends heard about it and wanted to come the next year.

"By year four, we had twenty-four people, so we had to set up another table. People became very attentive to whether they got to sit at the 'big' table for fourteen, or what they began calling 'the kids' table,' which was a piece of plywood on two saw horses. Both tables had nice tablecloths, good china, and silver. But as the party continued over the years, people got the idea that they didn't want to be assigned to 'the kids' table' two years in a row, so my husband and I spent a lot of time deciding who was going to sit next to whom, and that always changed at the very last minute when someone cancelled or someone's date changed.

"One guest always said that this was such an easy party because all I had to do was 'iron the table cloth and make the coffee.' Another said, 'Great party but you make the guests bring the damn dinner!' These statements continued to be quoted for years, and everyone laughed because our guests knew we weren't stressed about giving the party—we love to have people over.

"But no one realized how much effort it took to set up and clean up. So when we moved out of town, a friend offered to host so the party could continue. But she's a person who gets stressed about entertaining. Afterward she said she wouldn't do it again, because it was 'way too much work!'"

BREAKFAST WITH THE PARTY BITCH

Louise, a Southern lady who lives in a small town in Virginia, discovered that The Bitch can be as intimidating at breakfast as at dinner. Like many Southerners, Louise loves to entertain. But as anyone who grew up in the South knows, when company is coming, the pressure is on. In fact, Louise's cousin gave her a book titled *Being Dead Is No Excuse*, which says that if your own funeral buffet is tacky, if the tea sandwiches are soggy, or your relatives serve cheap cookies instead of petit fours, it would be so mortifying that you would die a second death.

Despite this social pressure and the fact that she has a full-time job and a limited budget, Louise frequently gives dinner parties for six or eight friends. So, when her minister announced his retirement, Louise volunteered to host a good-bye breakfast for his wife, asking for a guest list of her twenty closest friends.

But as the date grew closer, more and more parishioners found out about the breakfast and wanted to come. The Bitch wouldn't let Louise turn anyone away, even though she knew her home wasn't large enough to accommodate more than twenty guests.

When the number grew to fifty, Louise started waking up in the middle of the night being tortured by The Party Bitch warning, "You don't have enough plates and cups and glasses. Even if you borrow them, you'll have to wash them all. You *should* hire help—that's how everyone handles a lovely, big party, even though you're in debt up to your ears since you bought your new car. You don't have enough casserole dishes for the hot egg dish you were planning to serve—and you would probably trip and spill it all over the carpet on your way into the dining room anyway."

These are just a few of the ways The Party Bitch made Louise feel overwhelmed as the breakfast date approached. But The Bitch wouldn't let her ask for help, because her mother's favorite phrase kept running through her head: "You made your bed, now lie in it!"

And then the midnight catastrophic thinking began: How will you go to work if you have to wash all those dishes? Fifty juice glasses, fifty plates, fifty cups, fifty saucers, fifty linen napkins—you will have to use vacation days that you wanted to save to visit your children.

Finally, ten days before the party, Louise confronted her Bitch with the voice of reason. She decided she didn't care if people thought she was tacky: The only way she could serve fifty people breakfast was to use paper napkins, cups, and plates, plus plastic glasses and utensils! She would serve fresh strawberries, sliced oranges, and grapes instead of a complex fruit salad. She would buy and bake breakfast cakes and muffins instead of making hot casseroles. If you think this was a no-brainer instead of revolutionary, you probably aren't a middle-aged woman who runs with the country club set in a small Southern town.

The minute Louise decided to entertain the easy way, the pressure was off and she began to recapture her joy in giving the party. As usual, if the hostess is relaxed and happy, guests enjoy themselves. And Louise could tell by the decibel level at her breakfast that everyone was having a good time, standing around, chatting and laughing.

As the guests left, most told her they had a good time and that the party was "perfectly lovely." They complimented the way her flowers matched the pretty paper plates and napkins. They said it was creative the way she put her plastic forks and knives in cut glass bowls.

But a couple of ladies snarked that the party was "perfectly nice," which were code words for *tacky*. But Louise smiled when she heard this and said, "Well, bless your heart," which Southern ladies from Virginia can interpret to mean, "I hope you trip and break your nose on the way to your car."

Louise felt a little guilty for being ecologically incorrect as she threw all the paper and plastic into garbage bags at the end of the party. But mostly she felt relieved—and unafraid to give a big party again, especially since she, like most of the guests, had had a good time.

As the minister's wife left, she thanked Louise and confided that she had been nervous about the party because she was afraid that "maybe no one would want to come to say good-bye." But being a Southern lady *and* a minister's wife, even if she knew a Bitch when she heard one, she'd be much too proper to ever use that term.

HORRIBLE HOUSEGUESTS

A few summers ago, the *New York Times* ran an article about people who have summer homes in the Hamptons and tolerate obnoxious houseguests. There seemed to be two basic types: freeloaders and complainers. The freeloaders would arrive with a cheap or obviously re-gifted house gift and then expect to be fed all weekend. They would drink all the expensive wine and liquor without even buying a bottle of Two-Buck-Chuck. The worst case was a guest who arrived and then wouldn't leave for weeks until the homeowner paid for her train ticket home.

Then there are the complainers who don't like the food, think the bed is too hard, and act irritable if they are asked to help cook or clean up. One friend of mine told me that a guest, who spent a weekend at her house on the water, was indignant when asked to help prepare vegetables for dinner. "But this is my vacation!" the guest protested. New Yorkers are famous for being assertive, but many have such a raging Bitch in their heads that they let guests treat them like servants.

Since that time, I have heard from people all over the country about how houseguests can be hellish and how The Bitch makes them put up with bad behavior in their own homes. For example, a thirty-two-year-old newlywed, Lisa, who lives in Texas, told me this:

"I had heard many stories about the fun my husband had growing up with a cousin before her family moved to New Mexico. So when she moved back and bought a house two hours away from us, I invited her and her husband and two-year-old to come for a weekend. The first thing they did when they walked in was ask where the washing machine was, because they had brought a big laundry bag full of dirty diapers.

"Then they complained because I didn't have organic detergent. Then they were upset that I didn't have organic food. They didn't want to feed their little boy and put him to sleep before we had our dinner, so we had to make dinner very early and everything was completely chaotic. They made no attempt to fit into our lives or do what we wanted to do. They were supposed to stay for a long weekend but left in a huff a day early because we didn't want to go to a baby animal farm."

Part of Lisa was relieved when her difficult guests left early, but her Bitch was making her feel bad, telling her that she was a terrible hostess. So she called her mother. Instead of being sympathetic, her mom gave a Bitch-encouraging response: "Well, a hostess is supposed to make her guests feel comfortable. What did you do wrong?"

BANISHING THE BITCH

The desire to please can be a great asset and can help you to be a gracious hostess and charming guest. But if your Bitch turns this into an out-of-control *need*, entertaining can become a nightmare.

Of course we want our guests to say, "You shouldn't have worked so hard!" rather than implying we should have done more. Of course when we call our mother or friend and complain about a bad guest, we want her to say that we were completely in the right, rather than, "What did you do wrong?" But the world doesn't always back us up. And The Bitch never does.

This chapter has given you some concepts and tools to help you battle The Party Bitch. And here are a few more:

Get real about your "bad" behavior. Unless you threw up on the hostess or mooned the guests, your behavior was probably not bad enough to make you pull the covers over your head and say, "Ashamed!" But if you often feel this way or you find that you have been wearing beer goggles, you are probably drinking too much. Know your limit and stop there. Find ways to outsmart The Bitch when she tries to encourage you to have "just one more."

Know your limits. Be aware of your own limits not just in terms of how much to drink, but in terms of what kind of entertaining makes you comfortable. Keep the number of guests, the kind of food, and the type of party below your stress level. If you just want to invite people to your house for beer and hot dogs, that's fine. If you want to just invite them to a picnic in the park and make a basket full of sandwiches, that's fine, too. I know a literary agent who decided to throw a "fifties dinner" and served TV dinners and Jell-O. Everyone thought it was a hoot, not realizing that her Bitch made her afraid to cook.

While TV dinners may be a bit extreme for most people, one patient told me, "Once I realized that most people just want a night out with their friends, I stopped being nervous. If the hostess is having fun, it doesn't matter if the house is dusty and she serves pizza." Her friends love to come over when she makes a hearty soup on Sundays served with salad, crusty bread, and a dessert from a bakery. Now that she entertains in such an easy way, she enjoys her Sunday dinners as much as her guests.

Stop trying to be Martha Stewart. The woman who serves Sunday soup said she used to think everything had to be complicated and perfect. Whew! Some people like emulating Martha Stewart and enjoy entertaining like that. But it overwhelms most of us. So enjoy the beauty and creativity of Martha's magazine, but be clear with yourself about whether or not entertaining like that would make you crazed.

And don't feel you have to make all the food for your guests, especially if the recipes are complicated. Don't feel you have to make elaborate decorations or party favors. In fact, I have found that if you serve a multi-course gourmet meal, many people will be so intimidated by their Party Bitch that they won't invite you back to their house.

I know a bride who felt she "should" make goodie bags of homemade cookies for her wedding guests to take home. Anyone who has ever been married knows that only The Bitch would suggest that a bride has hours and hours of time to bake the week before her wedding. She was in a complete frazzle by the time she bagged the last cookie.

The point is that most guests like to come to a dinner or party just for the company and the night out. They won't mind if you buy most of the food or just serve something easy like roast chicken or grilled fish. They will be happy to bring a course. Only The Bitch would say that gourmet food is more important than a relaxed hostess—or bride.

12

BITCH-A-PHOBIA

She's Really Scary

The Bitch makes everyone afraid of something, but phobias are a whole other level of fear. Thunder, for example, which seems relatively benign to most people, can send a phobic person into a panic. The Bitch can even make a thunder phobic dread summer because that's when most thunderstorms occur.

I use the example of thunder because it illustrates a few features of phobias. First, phobias are irrational. As in this case, thunder never hurt anyone. It accompanies lightning, but lightning isn't what's feared. Second, even if it were fear of lightning, the chance of getting hit by lightning is minuscule. But simply using reason and logic doesn't cure phobic fear.

A fear of something as innocuous as frogs can make a person avoid any area where there even *might* be a frog—and that's almost everywhere. In severe cases, the person is so fearful of leaving home and encountering a frog that they stay in their house most of the time.

There are literally hundreds of kinds of phobias, everything from Ablutophobia (fear of bathing) to Zelophobia (fear of jealousy). I have mentioned some in previous chapters like fear of public speaking and social phobias caused by The Party Bitch. So this chapter will talk about other common phobias and how to cure them.

HYPOCHONDRIA

The day Woody Allen's movie *Midnight in Paris* (2011) opened to glowing reviews, my husband and I were walking down a quiet street in Manhattan. Headed toward us was what appeared to be an old man, so frail he seemed to be desperately hanging on to his young caretaker as he hobbled in our direction. The man had a wide-brimmed hat that hung over his face, so it wasn't until he was ten feet away that we realized it was Woody Allen clutching the arm of his wife, Soon Yi Previn. On a day when he should have been reveling in success and happiness, his well-documented Sick Bitch was spoiling it all.

Woody Allen has made us all chuckle at his fears. In fact, if I hadn't seen how truly miserable they made him, I would be laughing at his description of hypochondria, too:

"At the appearance of the mildest symptom, let's say chapped lips, I instantly leap to the conclusion that the chapped lips indicate a brain tumor. Or maybe lung cancer. In one instance I thought it was Mad Cow."

Woody says, "Every little ache or pain sends me to a doctor's office in need of reassurance," but medical consultations don't quiet his Sick Bitch. As he explains, "How can I relax knowing that the minute I leave the doctor's office, something may start growing in me and by the time a full year rolls around, my chest x-ray will look like a Jackson Pollock?"

At one time or another, The Bitch has made many of us worry that our mammogram will reveal that cancer is ravaging our breasts, or wonder if our persistent headache means we have a brain tumor. Perhaps because such fears are so common, experts can't agree on what percent of the population has true hypochondria, like Woody. I've read estimates that claim from 2 to 10 percent of people are hypochondriacs. But no matter how many people have this problem, everyone can agree that it's too painful to live with and needs to be cured.

To find out how to get that Sick Bitch out of our heads, I consulted the man who literally wrote the book on the subject, *Worried Sick?*. Dr. Fredric Neuman oversees one of the only clinics in the country devoted to curing hypochondria, located at his Anxiety and Phobia Center at the White Plains Hospital in White Plains, New York.

"When some people get anxious," Dr. Neuman told me, "they express their anxiety in physical symptoms like back pain or stomach aches. Then they begin worrying that these symptoms may have some obscure or devastating consequence like a brain tumor, pancreatic cancer, or AIDS.

"As a rule, the young people who worry about AIDS are not the ones who are engaging in risky sex. I had a man become worried because his girlfriend slept with someone else, and there was a police officer who obsessed about it just because he had to fingerprint someone who looked disheveled.

"I just gave you two examples of men, but the statistics are about fifty-fifty. As many women as men are hypochondriacs.

"Hypochondriacs check their health all the time. But the more they check, the more they worry. They go to the doctor all the time, asking for reassurance or medication, but this never lasts or works.

"They think they should avoid studying the disease they worry about, thinking that the more they know, the more symptoms they will invent. But at the Center we tell them to study the disease. As they learn more, they feel better, because they are confronting the fear and checking out the reality."

There are a number of fears that underlie hypochondriasis: fear of germs and contamination, fear of death, and fear of being alone and helpless. Whatever it is, Dr. Neuman advises patients to worry about it for forty-five minutes a day. They should fully imagine the scenario that scares them, such as: "The doctor tells you, 'I hate to break this terrible news, but . . .'"

Phobic people feel terrified by the scenario and stop there. But Dr. Neuman, like other therapists, forces them to continue by asking, "What would happen after the feared diagnosis? Then what? And then what?" By fully facing the depth of their fears and seeing how they would handle the worst possible scenario, The Bitch can't scare them anymore. And, as Dr. Neuman said, "Honestly, I think they get bored with the whole thing if they truly spend forty-five minutes a day thinking about it, rather than just feeling the fear for a moment and pushing it away."

He continued, "I do intense exposure therapy to whatever disease the person is worried about. Let's say it's leukemia. I tell them their chances of getting it are 1 in 10,000. But they say, 'What if I am the 1?'

"So I take them down to the cancer ward. We always follow-up a 'what if?' worry with 'well, then.'" I show them what kinds of treatment we offer to leukemia patients and they learn that even if they get the diagnosis, it's not hopeless. Ironically, people who really get the cancer they have worried about all their life stop worrying—they don't have to spend their life in fear of the diagnosis anymore. And they work with the chemotherapy and treatment."

SYMBOLIC REASONS FOR FEAR AND PAIN

For several years, a cardiologist sent me patients who were sure they were having heart attacks. While each felt terrible pain, there was no medical cause.

Psychotherapy quickly uncovered the cause of the pain: In every case, the patient was suffering emotional heartache. Someone they loved dearly had died, or had left them. Their Bitch said they shouldn't tell anyone how much they were suffering, but their bodies forced them to acknowledge their pain in a vividly symbolic way. Once they talked about their hurt and loss in therapy, their heart pain subsided over time.

The one exception was a woman who knew why she felt, as she said, "literally stabbed in the heart." After her son died, her beloved daughter-in-law would no longer talk to her. I suggested a three-month dose of an antidepressant, Lexapro. That removed the physical feeling of a knife in her heart, so that she was able to acknowledge her feelings of betrayal, and how the double loss of her son and daughter-in-law left a huge hole in her life. Then she could get on with the task of filling the hole, rather than just having The Bitch force her to rehash her hurt in an endless circle of pain.

Since that time, I have always checked to see if there might be a symbolic, psychological cause for pain that can't be medically explained. Patients suffering from neck pain are usually dealing with someone who is "a pain in the neck." Back pain is often explained because the person wishes someone would "get off my back." As long as their Bitch makes them unable to confront the real problem, she takes it out on their bodies.

A colleague who was trained in psychoanalysis once told me that my need to recheck that the stove was turned off every time I left the house meant that I was afraid my rage would burn the house down. Hmmm. I get mad at my husband sometimes, but not *that* mad.

So, while not every fear has a symbolic reason, many have hidden ones. For example, a man who always had a mild bridge phobia came into treatment when his promotion to manager required him to cross a long bridge to get to his new office. As I began a standard phobia treatment, his fear of bridges became worse. So I knew something else was going on.

It turned out that he was really afraid that he was incapable of being a good manager. So his subconscious Bitch told him that if his bridge phobia kept him from crossing the river, he wouldn't have to risk failing and being fired from his new job.

Luckily, while we worked on his underlying fear of failure, I told him to sing as he crossed the bridge each day. For some reason, it's very difficult to sing and be afraid at the same time. So he belted out Broadway show tunes while crossing the Hudson. Happily, he soon discovered that he was a far better manager than singer.

OTHER PHOBIAS

As I said at the beginning of this chapter, phobias are irrational. The Bitch blows danger way out of proportion. With a dog phobia, for example, what's the likelihood that you're going to get bitten by, much less lose your leg to, a cock-a-poo? But rational arguments don't help—even if you know exactly what caused the phobia—because The Bitch makes fear trump reason.

Being forced to confront the fear head-on also doesn't work. For example, if you're afraid of swimming, it will only get worse if someone throws you in the deep end yelling, "Sink or swim!" You might splutter your way to safety, but you won't feel calmer about jumping into the pool again.

In the early years of psychotherapy, professionals thought that to cure a phobia, you had to trace it back to its roots. Then two psychologists watched as a phobia developed in a child and realized that in most cases the root could never be found.

They brought this child, known as "little Albert," to their lab to enjoy playing with the white rats there. Albert showed no fear of the rats until a loud noise startled him and made him cry. After that, he was afraid of the rats because, in psychological terms, he "paired" his fear of the loud noise with them.

Soon, the psychologists noticed that Albert became afraid of anything with white fur. And then they saw that his fear had generalized to anything white. Since Albert's fear began before he could talk, and since it had spread far beyond the original "root," if the psychologists had not seen what caused Albert's white phobia, they would have never known. But it didn't matter. It was soon discovered that phobias could be cured without knowing where they started.

So if you have no idea why The Bitch is torturing you about dogs, snakes, heights, or thunder, no problem. The treatment of choice is a step-by-step coping method called progressive exposure, where you expose yourself to what you fear in gradual degrees, starting with the least frightening part first. For example, with a dog phobia you might start approaching a tiny, friendly puppy and work your way up to patting large breeds. But only when you get to a point where you can calmly handle your small fears—like a little puppy—do you gradually work your way up to larger, feared situations, like befriending a pit bull.

Some therapists teach you relaxation methods so you can calm yourself as you progressively face what frightens you. Others, like Dr. Neuman, say this isn't necessary. But as he told me, "Even Freud said that the way to get over a phobia was to get out of the office and be exposed to the fear."

Whether you are working with a therapist or want to try to desensitize yourself, I suggest that you begin by creating what is called a "hierarchy of fears." This means figuring out what makes your fear worse and what makes it better. So, for example, if you have a fear of being in an elevator, the longer you are in the elevator, the scarier it probably feels. But you would also want to recognize whether it makes it worse or better to have people in the elevator with you. And is it better or worse if you know the people? If they are men or women? Old or young? By learning as much as you can about your fear, you begin to feel like you have some handle on it.

So let's just say you are most comfortable in empty elevators. You would begin by using your skills to relax your mind and body. Then you might simply ride from the lobby to the first floor at a time when there are very few people around. When you can do that comfortably, you would ride up to the second floor in an empty elevator. You would continue this process until you could ride to the top of the Empire State Building in a crowded elevator while thinking about enjoying the fabulous view, instead of worrying about crashing and screaming.

Here's another example of how a therapist treated a woman with a snake phobia. (And no, snake phobias usually are not phallic.) The therapist started by having the woman read about snakes and get the facts about them. Then she looked at picture books of snakes. After she was comfortable looking at all the pictures, she handled toy snakes.

Toys were followed by a trip to the zoo, where she could look at a lot of real snakes. Then a trip to the pet store got her even closer to live snakes until she was ready to handle a small one.

When the woman actually handled a snake, she dropped it and was pleased and relieved to know that the snake wanted to wriggle away from her as fast as possible. She had always feared that snakes would leap at her from the ground and, typically, by avoiding snakes, she had also avoided discovering that her fear was unrealistic.

AIRPLANES

Airplane phobias are very common, but contrary to what you might think, The Bitch doesn't make most people afraid of crashing. Instead, she makes people afraid of having a panic attack and embarrassing themselves. They imagine themselves locked in a flying tube and losing control: falling down, screaming, or throwing up while all the other passengers stare at them and think they are crazy.

"I tell people to think of an airplane as a huge, flying movie theater," says Dr. Neuman. "Watch movies and distract yourself until you land. If you get uncomfortable, just like in a theater, you can get up and walk around or go to the bathroom.

"Sometimes people do throw up. That's why there are those vomit bags. But you never see people throwing up because they had a panic attack. And if they did, it would not be the end of the world."

If you have an airplane phobia, before you board the huge, flying movie theater, a therapist would take you (or you could take yourself) through a series of progressive steps to expose yourself to airplanes, just like in the snake example. You would read about airplanes and the statistics showing that flying is the safest form of travel. Then you could play with toy airplanes. After that, you could drive to the airport and walk around, imagining how much fun it would be to fly off to Disneyland or Paris.

When The Bitch puts an image in your mind of the plane crashing, tell her how extremely unlikely that would be. When she makes you think of running, screaming down the center aisle, immediately substitute an image of you relaxing on the plane with a nice drink and the leisure time to watch a movie or read a book.

Some airlines even work with people who are afraid of flying, letting them talk to pilots and visit a cockpit. Then you can take a short flight before you venture on a long one. And don't feel it's a cop-out if you have to take an anti-anxiety pill to go up, up, and away.

While fear of flying is no harder to treat than any other phobia, it can have a high relapse rate. Why? Because once you go through progressive exposure and take a flight, it's usually a long time before you fly again, so the fear can build up if you're not careful. It's not like getting over your fear of dogs, and then being able to reinforce your new comfort every day as you walk through town.

But just as with any other phobia, every time you see a plane flying through the air or see a picture of one in a movie or magazine, think how well you handled your fear of flying and anticipate how much fun it will be to fly away again.

EARTHQUAKES

I asked a psychotherapist in San Francisco how she helped people deal with fears of earthquakes and was surprised by her answer: "Everybody is in denial out here. Being afraid of earthquakes in California is like being afraid of snow if you live in Vermont." This statement proves Dr. Neuman's point that true phobias are always irrational.

But what if you have a rational fear of earthquakes? The difference between any rational fear and a phobia is that it is easier to calm rational fears with action plans.

An actress living in Los Angeles told me that she was afraid of earthquakes for a while. She and her husband, who was also an actor, considered moving but decided they had to stay in Los Angeles because it was where they found work. So they took the best precautions they could: They designated a place to meet in case of an earthquake and a person out of state whom they could call if they were separated or couldn't get to their meeting place. They also always keep a six-pack of water, a pair of tennis shoes, a blanket, and some protein bars in the trunks of their cars.

Whenever a fear of earthquakes pops into the actress's mind, she tells herself that she is prepared and tries to concentrate on something else. As she told me, "I act like that song from *The King and I*: I whistle a happy tune and soon I forget that I'm afraid."

Similarly, when I asked the psychotherapist in San Francisco what people were afraid of in her area, she told me this: "Marin County has the highest percentage of breast cancer in the country, and many people believe that the increased carcinogens in the environment are the culprit. BPA in plastics has been implicated, as well as hormones in milk and food.

"Just like earthquakes, anybody truly phobic would probably move. But people with this realistic fear can take precautions and attempt to avoid danger where possible. They use glass or metal water bottles and try to buy organic milk and food."

Once you have your action plan, if The Bitch tries to stir up your fear, you can just tell yourself that you have a plan and push the fear out of your mind using some of the techniques described below.

BANISHING THE BITCH

Even if The Bitch is making you terrified of something, don't let her tell you that nothing can be done about it. Phobias can be cured with cognitive and behavioral techniques described in this chapter. They may seem simplistic when you first hear about them, but therapists can attest to the fact that they are very effective. And here are some more:

Become an expert not only in what you fear but also about phobias. For example, anyone with hypochondria might want to read Dr. Neuman's book on the subject, *Worried Sick?*, which is not just a text but a workbook. And then study the specific treatments and symptoms of the disease you are afraid of having. Dr. Neuman warns that at first when you read about a disease, your anxiety will rise. But the more you know about it, the less it can scare you—especially if you counter every "what if?" with a realistic plan.

Also, make a deal with yourself to confine your worries to a specific time of the week. When a fear or worry pops into your head, write it down, put it in your worry folder, and don't look at it until the specific day and time you have designated to review your fears.

Once a week, at your specific worry time, pull out your folder, sort your worries into categories, and see which should be attended to and which were unfounded. Make plans to take action for the worries that need attention and rip up the other ones.

Apply Cognitive Behavior Therapy to help you manage your fear. Cognitive Behavior Therapy (CBT) is at the forefront of current treatment for anxiety and anxiety-related problems like phobias. The cognitive part is basically training yourself to think in a different way in order to combat your fear, and talking to yourself in ways that calm rather than inflame the fear.

CBT includes very simple but effective strategies like:

- Self-coaching: Tell yourself things like, "You can do it. Just take it slow. Nothing is going to hurt you. You have nothing to fear but fear itself."
- Distraction: Get up and do something instead of focusing on your fear. Call a friend, listen to music, or go to the gym. Do anything that engages you.
- Imagery: Imagine yourself smiling, relaxed, and pleased with yourself when you have overcome your fear.

The behavior therapy part uses techniques like deep breathing and relaxation to calm your mind and your body before and after taking steps to expose yourself to fear. It is very effective to learn a relaxation technique and use it whenever you even think of whatever scares you, so you can do the opposite of what little Albert did: you will "pair" relaxation with your fear to get rid of it.

Remember that mental health is not the absence of fear. Mental health is acting in the face of fear. Sometimes we grow out of a fear and it becomes a barely remembered part of our past. For example, when a friend of mine was a little girl, she "needed" to have all her toys lined up on her dresser in a very specific order. "If anyone changed that order, I would get hysterical and throw a fit," she told me. "But I grew out of it and don't need to be that orderly anymore."

However, if your phobia or compulsion has followed you into adulthood, it may never go away completely, but it doesn't have to constrict your life. Congratulate yourself on each step you take to combat your phobia; pat yourself on the back every time you act in the face of the fear. The goal is to get to a point where fears and phobias no longer dominate your thoughts and your life.

13

SICK BITCH

Some of It's in Your Head

When you receive a bad diagnosis, it's natural to feel fearful, depressed, and angry. Then, if The Bitch lets you, you begin to adjust and start doing whatever the doctor suggests to combat the disease or injury.

Although a positive attitude doesn't necessarily cure, it makes life as pleasant as possible. But The Sick Bitch tries to keep you stuck in fear, endlessly imagining bad outcomes. And she tries to add guilt, saying that you caused the illness, either by something you did or didn't do, or because your personality made you prone to the disease.

It can be helpful to find a role model: someone who wrestled with the same illness in a way that you admire. So, this chapter will present a number of positive role models, as well as Bitch-defeating approaches to sickness and health.

"CATASTROPHIZERS" VERSUS "MINIMIZERS"

Before we talk about illness, let's talk about staying healthy. And the best way to do that—as you well know—is to eat and drink in a healthy manner, exercise regularly, and get check-ups. But The Bitch often makes you forget that there's another important item on that list: to take your doctor's advice.

Physicians complain that too many patients either minimize their problems or turn them into catastrophes. Catastrophizers get panicky at the very thought of a physical exam. Their Sick Bitch tells them that the results are going to be so horrible that they often avoid the exam altogether. If they get themselves to the doctor's office, anxiety causes their hearts to race so fast that it's impossible to get an accurate blood pressure reading. Their Sick Bitch makes them sure that every mammogram is going to reveal incurable cancer or that their irregular periods mean they will never be able to have children.

On the other hand, The Bitch tells minimizers not to pay any attention to serious symptoms; if you don't think about it, it will go away. So they ignore vaginal bleeding or lumps in their breasts. They won't treat serious osteoporosis because they have read newspaper reports about a rare side effect of medication. Or, like Steve Jobs, they treat their cancer with unproven alternative medicine until the disease is too advanced for traditional medicine to cure it.

One gynecologist with a New York City practice described the situation this way: "Maybe some of the problem has to do with location: My practice is heavily weighted toward anxious urbanites whose hobby seems to be worrying and complaining. They are sure every little symptom spells disaster. A colleague of mine in rural Wisconsin who sees strong, silent farm women told me his patients are the opposite: They claim they are too busy to come in for an exam. They ignore pain and symptoms until their cancers are very advanced.

"We all long for more patients who take care of their health without getting hysterical. If I tell them something looks abnormal, they have it checked out. If something is wrong, they have it treated. If it's nothing, they forget it and go on with their lives. They can put things in perspective."

SEXUALLY TRANSMITTED DISEASES (STDS)

That same gynecologist says she also wishes more young women could put social diseases in perspective, too. "These days if you are sexually active, you are going to get exposed to human papilloma virus and herpes. That's just a fact of life and shouldn't interfere with relationships."

But it does. I am thinking of two patients of mine who had herpes. In each case, The Sick Bitch made them feel awful.

The younger woman, a pretty blonde sales executive in her twenties I'll call Karen, discovered that she had herpes and told the man she was dating, assuming that he gave it to her. He denied it vehemently and stopped seeing her immediately, saying that he didn't want to date anyone with a "social disease."

The other woman, a forty-five-year-old goldsmith I'll call Jewel, was upfront with men: letting them know that she had suffered from herpes for many years but rarely had an outbreak. She assured them she would let them know if she did, so they could take precautions. Over the years, she accepted the fact that some men didn't want to deal with it and some men didn't seem to mind.

But what devastated Jewel was that a man she had been happily dating for six months, a man she thought might be a keeper, suddenly announced that he "couldn't have a serious relationship with anyone with a disease like herpes."

Both Karen and Jewel were devastated because each thought she had found a caring relationship. In both cases, their Bitches tried to convince them that what their boyfriends implied was true: they were dirty, diseased tramps. It took therapy for each woman to regain her self-respect and the courage to date again.

Karen's Bitch tried to get her to take revenge on men, saying, "Your boyfriend gave you herpes, so why risk rejection by revealing your condition to the next guy?" But through therapy, she realized that if she didn't tell in the beginning, a man would be justified in being angry when she finally decided to be honest. Karen bypassed her fear of rejection by using a dating website for people with herpes. She found her husband that way.

Jewel also struggled to decide whether to be honest about her herpes, since she rarely had a contagious outbreak of sores. She cried as she told me that her boyfriend "made me feel like an 'untouchable,' like I had leprosy or syphilis or something."

"Actually," I told Jewel, "it's your Bitch making you feel that way." Soon she realized that her ex-boyfriend was commitment phobic, looking for any excuse to leave her as he had left all his previous girlfriends. She, like Karen, decided that honesty was a good test of potential mates. Both found someone to love them as they are.

STRESS-RELATED DISEASE

Even if you have a disease that is stress related, or something like lung cancer or heart disease that's caused by smoking, don't let The Bitch beat you up about it. What's done is done. You can't go back in time and change past behavior. Instead, work to stay as healthy, positive, and stress free as you can from now on.

While there is no evidence that a positive attitude cures illness, it surely makes life easier. Research shows that psychotherapy and support groups can help keep you positive and thus reduce tension, fatigue, anxiety, and depression, confounding The Bitch and improving quality of life.

Dr. Mary Travis is a psychologist who leads a support group for cardiac patients who have had defibrillators implanted in their chests. She revealed some of the ways The Bitch tortures people in her group.

"People who have had heart attacks usually go through a period of anxiety and depression. When they get a defibrillator, it's proof that they have a chronic heart problem that's not going to get better.

"Some people get so anxious that they tell themselves, 'I can't do *anything* that might set it off. I shouldn't garden or drive.' They put unnecessary restrictions on themselves beyond what their cardiologist tells them, diminishing their enjoyment of life.

"There's a lot of self-blame—'I shouldn't have smoked,' [or] 'I shouldn't have eaten badly.' Maybe that's true, but it's not productive to carry this on and on. The other people in the group help them get on a more positive track.

"They also help each other learn to manage stress, because stress management is key, especially for people who are very intense. They have to learn to let some things go. Learning brief meditation strategies and mindfulness helps keep anxiety and anger in check during everyday activities.

"Sometimes The Bitch will tell them, 'You don't have to take your medication.' It's like the devil on their shoulder, but again, the group helps set them straight."

Dr. Travis says that the Bitch-free people say things like, "I've faced death, so I don't sweat the small stuff." They have an appreciation for life and how unimportant little stresses are.

DIABETES

Diabetes is often known as a silent killer, because the symptoms can be so mild that adults often don't realize that they have the disease until it's quite progressed. But if left untreated, they can go blind, die of kidney disease, or need amputations. Diabetes is one of the fastest growing diseases, both the adult version and also the type that affects children, which rose 21 percent between 2001 and 2009.

People who are diagnosed with diabetes as adults can be vulnerable to The Bitch blaming them for "causing" the disease by having a poor diet or being overweight. But even those who get diabetes as a child can be tortured by their Bitch.

Jessica Schlenoff is a private tutor in her thirties who lives in San Francisco. She told me that, when she was a child, she began "having strange symptoms: weight loss, thirst, hunger, and fatigue. My best friend Carrie knew these were symptoms of diabetes.

"The night before I went to the doctor, my dad took me out for a nice dinner. For dessert, I had a chocolate truffle. I remember eating that truffle like it was yesterday, how it felt to bite into it, knowing it could be the last dessert I would have without having to think about the consequences. It was the last truffle I ever ate, and it still makes me want to cry thinking about it. I can taste it in my memory.

"When I got the diagnosis, I was afraid and flooded with how little I knew about the disease." Jessica had just seen the movie *Steel Magnolias* (1989) where the main character dies because she got pregnant as a diabetic, so her first question was whether she could have children.

"I can't separate myself from my diabetes since I got it when I was a child," she told me. "I get discouraged when my blood sugar spikes for no reason and I try so hard to be good. It hits me when I can't exercise or walk without worrying about low blood sugar. It affects me when I feel neuropathy and think about having to always live with this condition. When I feel healthy, though, it helps bring me out of the discouraging thoughts, and I am proud of how well I take care of myself.

"But I recently got a CGM [continuous glucose monitor] that is attached to me. I don't wear it all the time because it makes me self-conscious. I hate telling people I'm diabetic. Nobody really understands."

One way that Jessica "fights back" against The Bitch is by raising money for Walk to Cure Diabetes each October. Here is part of what she wrote last year as she solicited donations: "I still remember the day at age twelve, when I was told I had juvenile diabetes—the fear, the shock, and the eventual realization that my life would never be the same. That I would never truly be free again, burdened with multiple daily shots, blood tests, food restrictions, significant risks of blindness, heart disease, amputations, kidney failure, stroke, and death. Now, after approximately 15,000 injections and 40,000 blood tests, I can say that I have grown accustomed to being a Type 1 diabetic, even 'good' at working diligently to keep my blood sugar under control."

Jessica said that she raises money in hope of a cure so that "no child has to become 'good' at being a diabetic. I am fighting so that kids can just be good at being kids." The Bitch may make you feel like your disease is your fault, but you can ignore this voice by remaining positive and raising awareness like Jessica.

CANCER

You are in the doctor's office and you have just received the terrible news: you have cancer. Even if the doctor is reassuring, The Bitch screams, "Oh, my God! You are going to die a hideous death!" The healthy part of your brain knows you should be thinking, "I'm going to be one of the ones who beats this!" But you wonder how in the world you are going to keep your spirits up and keep up a good fight.

The next few weeks as you go through more diagnostic tests and plan a treatment, The Bitch will find many ways to torture you, but there are as many ways to counter her, so you don't have to feel sicker than you are.

Having a great role model helps show you the way to stay positive. So, let me tell you about a few of them.

Lynnette grew up singing country music. When this young mother found out that her mammogram revealed a lump and the biopsy revealed it was cancer, her first thoughts were, "Oh, my God! If I die, who will raise my little girls?" For a couple of weeks as she went through tests and considered treatment plans, she was so worried about her children that she couldn't think of anything else.

Then one day as she was absentmindedly thumbing through a stack of old records from when she was a child, Lynnette saw one that had been her favorite by Jerry Jeff Walker. As she told me, "All of a sudden I started to sing and dance with the music. It made me feel so much better. There was one particular song, 'Up against the Wall, Redneck Mother,' calling out a bad mother. I decided that cancer was my 'redneck mother,' and I was going to beat it. Every time I get depressed, I begin singing that song, and I feel stronger and determined to stay healthy for my girls."

Whatever works, go for it! Here is a completely different way a friend of mine defeated Sick Bitch fears and made the world better in the process.

Marge Schlenoff is a psychoanalyst and Jessica Schlenoff's mother. In 2003, when Marge was fifty-five, an oncologist told her she had advanced cancer and only one year to live. "I literally fell on the floor when I heard that," she said. "When I got home, I realized I wasn't afraid of dying. I was just afraid to die with regrets.

"I had had a successful career, a practice that helped people. I had raised two wonderful daughters, had a happy marriage, and I'd tried to lead a moral life. But I had the major feeling that I hadn't fully actualized myself. I knew I had the capacity to help people in a broader, deeper way than just my work and my family."

Thank goodness, Marge found out that there had been a misdiagnosis. While she had advanced cancer that had spread to her lymph nodes, there was "only" a tumor in one breast, not two. Her prognosis wasn't as dire as she had initially been told, but the feeling that she hadn't done all she could with her life persisted.

Marge felt she had a mission to fulfill but no idea what that mission was. So she started working on her bucket list of things she wanted to do before she died and hoped she would figure out her mission along the way.

"I was in treatment for a year and then, in 2005, I started on my list of things I had always wanted to do. First on that list was a trip to South Africa with my husband. Standing in Nelson Mandela's cell, we saw the mat on the floor where he spent twenty-six years. The fact that Mandela didn't get out of prison and say, 'Let's kill every person who put us in here' was miraculous. I was inspired to do something to help his country. That's how Teach with Africa started."

Teach with Africa—the organization that Marge and her husband, Larry, started in 2006 and incorporated for non-profit status in 2007—has helped thousands of students in South Africa and the United States through a teacher exchange program.

"The American teachers say it transforms their lives to learn about resilience: The African kids they teach are often living in shacks, having lost their parents to AIDS, but they have turned out to be capable people who have kept their strength and compassion. The stories and lessons the teachers bring back are important for kids in our country to learn.

"The African teachers learn about technology and how to integrate it into the classroom. They also learn about making lessons that incorporate many learning styles, since the primary way to teach there is still 'chalk and talk.' Teachers learn how to act out lessons or give children experiences that make what they are learning come alive."

I spoke to Marge in between her sessions with patients, a few days before a major fundraiser for Teach with Africa. It had been well over five years since her cancer treatment, so the risk of a relapse is way down. But she was much too happy and busy to even think about cancer anyway.

THE BUMPY ROAD TO RECOVERY

Sometimes the most difficult part of dealing with an illness or injury comes after the initial diagnosis, especially if you are facing a lengthy, painful, or difficult treatment and recovery.

Sometimes chemotherapy isn't too difficult to live with. Other times it can make a patient feel so sick and nauseated that The Bitch tells them "give up, it isn't worth it" even when the prognosis is good.

It can be the same with operations or injuries that require extensive, painful physical therapy. Knee replacement therapy and exercise regimens are so painful for some people that The Bitch tells them it isn't going to work so they might as well stop.

But if you hang in there, ignore the tempting Bitch siren song, and stick it out until you are fully cured, you're home free, right? Wrong! That's just when The Bitch begins to torture some people. Just as many soldiers are brave during battles but break down when they get home, some people with life-threatening illnesses often hold it together beautifully—until after treatment.

Susan Lewen, a director of development who lives in Connecticut, was shocked when that happened to her. The mother of two children, she decided when a routine mammogram revealed a very aggressive cancer that "I wasn't going to leave my kids until I was done raising them. So I was determined to do everything I needed to do to get well.

I had surgery, fifteen months of chemo, and then radiation. My toenails, fingernails, hair, and eyebrows fell off. But I look back on the e-mails I was sending and I was very chipper. I was very strong through the process, keeping track of all my meds and treatment and denying that I was going through something BIG.

"It was only after I was through the treatment and declared clear, that the emotional impact hit me. I felt a powerful fear that I had never felt before. Every time I got a little pain, I thought the cancer had recurred and spread to my bones. Every time I heard about someone dying or having a recurrence, I thought I would have one, too.

"I found a therapist who helped me acknowledge that I had been through something dramatic and traumatic, and to realize that someone who has gone through all that would be very susceptible to any story about suffering. Just acknowledging that I was very strong in spite of my fears helped. My therapist also helped me apply logic to see that just because fears came to mind, didn't mean I had to give in to them.

"Now, seven years out, I am proud to be a survivor. I can say to myself, 'Holy cow, you went through a lot,' and see myself as a person with a happy future."

LIFE IN A WHEELCHAIR

A very close friend of mine, Sharon Golub, was a psychologist with a family history of Parkinson's. Sharon's father was diagnosed with the disease in his fifties, so she knew that it could happen to her, too. But instead of letting The Bitch make her live in fear of a bad diagnosis, Sharon deliberately lived joyfully.

She loved having friends over to her house, especially in the summer when she served dinner beside her pool. She enjoyed her private practice and reveled in teaching, finding it especially gratifying to mentor students whose parents had not gone to college, nurturing them as professors had once nurtured her.

Sharon's first reaction to receiving her diagnosis was shame: She didn't want to become a burden to her husband and sons. She kept her diagnosis secret and, at first, only told her immediate family and two friends. I was honored to be one of them.

She was determined not to become an object of pity, but to continue to be the kind of person who enjoyed life, the kind of person that people enjoyed being around. And she also was determined to be a good role model for her family, knowing that the gene could have been passed on to her sons or grandchildren.

Although it was a terrible loss, Sharon retired before she became impaired and then had to give up her house when she needed to be in a wheelchair and have full-time help. But she did it all without complaint. Sure The Bitch tried to give her a "woe is me" approach and tried to make her focus on her problems. But as Sharon told me, "That wouldn't get me anywhere. So I'm going to focus on what I have and what I can do."

Have you ever tried to negotiate life in a wheelchair? It isn't easy. First there is the humiliation of either talking to people's bellybuttons or having them lean down to talk to you. Then there are the many places that still are not wheelchair accessible. Going out to restaurants was always tricky. Even when the door seemed relatively level with the sidewalk, we would usually have to ask some strong passersby to help lift Sharon over a little step. And the look on some maître d's faces let us know they were not pleased to have "disabled" people as patrons. Sharon usually ignored the sour looks, knowing her big smile would win over her waiter.

Sharon tried to replace what she lost with other pleasures. For example, when she had to stop dancing, she continued her love of music in other ways. She bought a keyboard and learned how to play the piano. She loved to sing, so she signed up for courses in nightclub and Broadway songs. When friends came for a visit, she would often want to sing with or for them.

People loved to visit Sharon. She was good company with good conversation. She was much more interested in hearing what was going on in your life than in telling you about hers. She kept up on the latest movies, plays, and books. She was a mediocre Scrabble player but loved the game and never seemed to mind losing. When she was no longer able to cook, she made sure that the caretaker she hired was a terrific chef who would help her continue to host lunches and dinners.

Sharon's caretaker told me, "She was very Zen like. I never heard her complain or raise her voice." How did she resist The Sick Bitch, who always provokes complaints, self-pity, and anger? "I know it won't get me anywhere," Sharon once told me. "No one wants to hear it, including me."

So the strongest complaints even her closest friends ever heard were things like, "This hasn't been a good day" or "This has been a bad week." When pressed for details, she would usually say, "Tell me something funny or interesting to distract me instead." So for months after her death, I was still thinking, "Oh, I have to tell Sharon that!"

One day she told me that the thing she hated most about having Parkinson's was that she never could be alone. Someone always had to be with her in case she fell or, in the later stages of her illness, to help her to get out of bed or go to the toilet. So in typical Sharon style, she worked out her upset over being constantly watched with art therapy: cutting out all the pictures of eyes she could find and making collages out of them.

Sharon was a sensual woman who loved the company of men. But her friends were skeptical when, late into her illness and confined to a wheelchair, after her husband died, Sharon announced that she would like to begin dating.

I often tell my patients that I have never known a woman who liked men and liked sex, who didn't find someone to date. But when Sharon told me that her new goal was to find a boyfriend, I figured I'd found the exception to my rule. But she proved me wrong—or was it that she proved me right? Anyway, the happy news is that she began dating a charming widower who brought her great joy until the day she died.

The temple was packed for Sharon's funeral. She had been a great role model for how to live a full and joyful life in spite of illness and The Sick Bitch. But as I was writing this, thinking that Sharon was as close to a saint as anyone could get, I decided to check with her son, David, the main person who coordinated her care toward the end of her life.

"My mother was an enormously proud woman, so it doesn't surprise me that she wouldn't complain to her friends. But believe me, she complained plenty and got cranky sometimes. People need outlets for these very human feelings, so I don't begrudge that I sometimes was her complaint sponge. It was part of the job.

"The key theme was ways in which the disease challenged her dignity: dependency, lack of bladder control, memory loss, long sleepless nights when she couldn't move enough to turn over. But after venting a bit, her mood would improve.

"Here's my take: aging is difficult. Disease is scary. Everybody needs to share the dark side with an intimate in order to process it all. I hope I handle the cards I get with the grace and dignity that she did. And I hope on my journey I have as wonderful, supportive, and loving friends as she did."

And I know all those friends hope our children will be as loving and supportive as David.

BANISHING THE BITCH

Illness or injury is a frightening experience even for people with great psychological and physical strength. The Bitch is bound to say things that, at least occasionally, make you feel weak and hopeless. So prepare to fight not just the illness, but Bitch negativity.

There will be days when you want to give up. The Bitch will tell you to postpone getting important diagnostic tests. She will catastrophize and tell you that you will never recover your health or mobility, so don't bother following through with treatment or therapy.

If you expect to want to give up occasionally, then you can plan to get the help and encouragement you need to face not just your illness, but also the dark days and moods that may accompany it.

No matter what the prognosis, try to live with joy. When you feel sick, even if you don't have a big Bitch, it's hard to think of anything except your fear and pain. It's easy to make life just revolve around visits to the doctor. But that's a terrible way to live.

Even if you've been given a bad diagnosis, actually, *especially* if you have been given a bad diagnosis, it's important to feel like you are "really living" every day. At the least, I recommend giving yourself daily treats and fun to counteract the fear and pain.

As a friend of mine told me when she received the diagnosis of aggressive breast cancer with a poor prognosis: "In my case, the whole thing makes me want to get up each morning and live every day to the fullest. I want to hug my kids, see my friends, enjoy the beauty of each day. It's totally cliché but true. That's the way I can deal with this."

Many women find support groups helpful—the one place they can let down their hair, even—and sometimes especially—if chemo has made them bald. I suspect the one place my friend Sharon felt perfectly free to complain was with the friends she made in her Parkinson's support group. If you are the kind of person who doesn't like groups, you can get some of the same kind of support through books like *Crazy Sexy Cancer Tips* where people with your disease talk about how they coped.

No matter what the prognosis, create your bucket list. A bucket list is a list of all the things you want to see and do before you die. Half the fun is creating it. The Bitch might make you superstitious and afraid—Oh, no! What happens if I do everything on my list? Does that mean I will die? No, it means that you will be lucky enough to create another list of things to do and see.

What if, like Marge Schlenoff, going to South Africa is top on your list, but you don't have the time or money, or you are too infirm to make a big trip like that? Outsmart The Bitch who is trying to make you feel sorry for yourself. Have the fun of planning the trip with travel books from your library. Then with movies from Netflix and videos from YouTube, you can go anywhere in the world via your computer.

14

THE BITCH IN
SOMEONE ELSE'S HEAD

Self-Protection

Sometimes a mean comment gets stuck in your head. When you're feeling low, The Bitch will repeat that remark and sap your self-confidence. Here are a few examples from different women:

An old boyfriend said, "You have such small eyes. That's why you're not beautiful." From then on, I doubted my looks until my little girl looked up at me one day and said, "Mommy, you have such pretty eyes."

Looking back, I realize I must have had some learning disabilities because I was always a slow reader and had a hard time with spelling. Words seemed to jump around on the page although there was nothing wrong with my eyesight. Once when my third-grade teacher asked me to come up and write something on the blackboard, I misspelled several words. All the kids laughed. I was humiliated. I still make spelling mistakes, and it makes me feel stupid.

My mother was germophobic, and every time I went into the kitchen, she would follow me around and criticize what I was doing. It made me feel stupid and dirty. Luckily, I had a wonderful grandmother who gave me hugs and told me I was a good girl.

I invited my grandmother to see my new house. I was so proud and excited until she said, "Don't worry, dear. One day you will get a *nice* house."

My sister had a face-lift before she moved to a new city. I was visiting one day, and she asked me to pick up her clothes from the cleaner.

When I gave her name, the cleaner said, "Are you her mother?" When I got back to her apartment, I told my sister. Instead of saying, "He must be crazy," she smiled and said, "How did that make you feel?" I have been self-conscious about my wrinkles ever since.

An architect spent a year as a volunteer overseeing the extensive renovation of her church. She did a fabulous job, but the comments that stick in her mind and distress her are the snarky ones: "Let me tell you what I would have done differently" or "I liked it better before."

Obviously, these are minor insults and cruelties. So you can imagine how extended verbal or physical abuse can leave a huge Bitch in someone's head, especially since cruel people often blame their victims. So this chapter presents women who have found the strength to stand up to toxic parents, classmates, spouses, and sometimes even whole societies. If they can stand up to all those Bitches, so can you.

TOXIC PARENTS

Who do you think you are?
You were behind the barn when the brains were passed out.
Why can't you be like her?
You're a bad girl!

Even good parents blurt out hurtful words occasionally, messages that can stay in your mind as The Bitch. But toxic parents are something else. They are neglectful or cruel and don't seem to notice or care.

When the playwright Wendy Wasserstein was a chubby little girl, her mother tried to get her to diet by saying, "Everyone is looking at you and thinking, 'Look at that fat girl!'" I have no idea whether her mother was being clueless or deliberately cruel. And I have no idea whether Wasserstein was constitutionally heavy or whether she just kept the weight on until the day she died as a conscious or unconscious "screw-you" to her mother.

But parental criticism doesn't end in childhood. A woman I know—with an MBA and a successful career in management consulting—had

parents who told her on her fortieth birthday that she was "a disappointment" because she had never married or had children. Instead of motivating her to give her parents the grandchildren they so desperately wanted,
The Bitch used their criticism to lower her self-esteem and keep her from
even dating.

Every psychologist hears examples of parents who are truly toxic:
insulting, hitting, or constantly comparing their child to others in a
negative way. And occasionally there are bone-chilling examples of
physical or sexual abuse.

Often the worse the parent is, the more the child blames herself. Why? Society tells us that parents are good. In storybooks, only
stepmothers are wicked. And religious institutions tell us to honor our
parents.

Furthermore, since it's impossible for young children to leave
home, they are trapped. So children blame themselves, hoping that if
they caused their parents' bad behavior, they might be able to do something to make it stop. But of course, a cruel parent is not going to change
no matter what the child does. So the cruelty becomes embedded as a
Bitch in the child's head.

Psychotherapy (and reading this book) can help. But sometimes the
cure is achieved by confronting the parent. Here are two examples of
patients who did that in my office:

I worked with a man I'll call Charles, who struggled in school with
an undiagnosed learning disability that made it hard for him to read. His
father hit him and told him he was "stupid" when he brought home
poor report cards. Despite this, Charles persisted and eventually graduated from high school and college.

When Charles became my patient, he was a respected middle
manager, but he still heard his father's voice in his head, saying "You're
so stupid!" whenever he made a mistake. And even though he was six
feet tall, he still felt like a child with a larger, more powerful father. So
I suggested that he bring his dad to my office and, with my support, tell
him that his criticism hurt even more than his beatings.

You can imagine my surprise when the "large, powerful father"
turned out to be a wizened old man—and a completely unrepentant
one, too. But even though Charles's father refused to apologize, defen-
sively claiming he was only trying to "beat some sense" into his son, in

my office Charles could finally see with new eyes that his father was just a small, misguided old man who was no longer a threat.

An equally Bitch-defeating confrontation took place when a woman, Françoise, who had grown up in Paris, brought her very chic French mother into my office. Françoise, a beautiful, successful woman, had tears in her huge brown eyes when she said, "I've tried all my life to please you, but you have *never* given me a compliment!"

I found this hard to believe until her mother said, "But of course I didn't give you compliments. You were very smart and pretty, and it was my duty as a mother to keep you from getting a swelled head." Françoise was still frustrated and angry, but The Bitch could no longer claim, "Your mother never loved you."

TOXIC CLASSMATES

Were you teased by the boys or tormented by the mean girls at school? If so, even if you graduated long ago, I bet your Bitch is still repeating some of the things they said.

A woman told me, "Some kids called me 'fat face' in first grade. I always cringed when I looked at a picture my parents had framed of me from that era. All I could see was this chubby girl with a fat face and socks drooping into the heels of her shoes. I tried to avoid looking at it, because I heard 'fat face' ringing in my ears.

"When I was cleaning out my parents' home after they died, somehow I saw what they saw in that picture: a cute little kid. Yes, maybe I was chubby, but I was also cute. It was like a burden was lifted. It was great to like the little kid I used to be."

There have always been mean boys and girls in school, but now there is a greater awareness of the genuine harm that bullying can inflict. In fact, there are laws to protect children from harassment. An ordinary mother from Georgia fought all the way to the Supreme Court to help not just her daughter, but to keep all kids from being harassed. It's one of my favorite stories from my book *Mother Power*, so I'll repeat it here:

A fifth-grade boy made repeated sexual comments and advances to a girl assigned to a seat next to him. When her mother complained to the teacher and then to the principal, she was ignored. The girl's grades fell, she had nightmares, and her father even found a suicide note, but it took three months just to get the boy's seat moved away.

The mother, a hospital clerk with only a high school education, was so angry about this that she went to the library every night to research sexual harassment. She hired an attorney to sue the school in an effort to ensure that schools would provide a harassment-free environment.

The suit went all the way to the Supreme Court where the justices at first seemed skeptical, asking how to draw the line between harassment and garden variety teasing and flirting. But in May 1999, the court agreed with the mother: students have a right to look to their teachers and schools for protection.

I love this story because it shows that although The Bitch would tell many parents, "How could *you* buck the whole school system? Who do you think you are?" the natural protectiveness of "mother power" can trump The Bitch!

TOXIC MARRIAGE

A female hedge fund manager who knows her investments, but nothing about domestic violence, told me, "Wife beating is a lower-class problem." That's one myth The Bitch uses to shame victims of domestic abuse. But the truth is very different. In fact, in Greenwich, Connecticut, one of the wealthiest towns in America, domestic abuse is the second most reported crime after burglary.

Priscilla Jeffrey is a hotline volunteer and victim advocate in Greenwich. She explained, "Many of the men here are powerful executives and CEOs. They are used to people saying yes to them and kowtowing. They are used to ordering people around and getting their way. They begin to treat their wives that way, and when the wives object, some of these guys hit them.

"Hitting is commonly acknowledged as abuse," Priscilla says, "but it can take other forms. Constant criticism, insults, or threats are also domestic violence. It's really anything that hurts someone else."

Regardless of socioeconomic status, the pattern of domestic abuse is usually the same. In the beginning, the man is incredibly charming. He is interested in everything the woman does and often brings flowers and gifts. But then he starts changing very slowly, so it's often hard to know when or how it started or realize how bad it's become.

As the criticism increases, both The Bitch and the abuser say it's deserved. The abuser begins to cut the victim's contact with friends and family and access to money through a job or bank account—all the better to control the woman, so when the battering starts, she not only feels ashamed but also helpless and alone. Now that professionals have identified this pattern, experts agree that any woman could get trapped in the slow, downward spiral of criticism, isolation, and abuse.

The director of the San Francisco Department on the Status of Women, Dr. Emily Moto Murase, with the full support of Mayor Edwin Lee, has instituted programs that serve as a shining example of how a city can reduce domestic violence. As she told me, "About ten women used to be killed each year, but for the last three and a half years, no one has died. Our community-based resources are reaching would-be victims early enough to prevent murder. The police still get 4,000 domestic violence reports, however, so there is still much work to be done."

The way the police handle these reports has changed radically, and this has led to a decrease in violence. "Years ago, the police used to listen to the batterer and just walk him around the block until he calmed down," Murase said. "Now the police listen to the person who was battered and recognize the batterer as someone who has broken the law.

"We have hotlines and three shelters that are always full. But instead of building more shelters, we have spent the money on prevention and early intervention, including outreach in many languages. Most communities, including ethnic and religious groups, often initially reject help, claiming the problem doesn't exist in their community." Leaders who want to cover up the problem believe The Bitch when she says, "What can you do?" or "This is a matter best left to the family." So Dr. Murase's department has had to come up with creative methods to reach battered women who are isolated at home, including those unable to speak English.

How would you reach such women? Dr. Murase explains one creative approach: "The one thing all these women do is shop for the food. So, for example, a community collaborative against domestic violence printed grocery bags in Chinese with information about how to get help. The grocery store owners were happy to use the bags because we gave them to grocers for free. As soon as this program started, the domestic violence hotline was flooded by Chinese callers."

The Bitch makes too many women and children believe what the abuser is saying—that it's their fault. But the pattern of abuse can be broken with a call to a hotline. Trained volunteers, often survivors of abuse, will accompany the victim to file police reports and offer support. But they don't judge a woman who is not ready to leave or press charges.

As one former victim who is now a volunteer counselor told me, "When I was in the middle of the abuse, I would have told you I couldn't make it on my own. I had been a teacher, but I had become isolated. I had started drinking to ease my pain. The key to getting out of the relationship was to stop drinking, go to AA, and get some support."

Here's the advice she gives to all women: "Abusers look for 'nice' women who won't complain when things start going bad. So don't be afraid to speak up and label bad behavior as 'mean.' Don't put up with it. Keep your own money, be sure to keep access to a bank account, and keep up your skills so you can earn a living." That seems like great advice for everyone.

TOXIC SOCIETY

Read the newspaper, listen to the news, open your eyes, and you will see that the world is full of poverty, hate, discrimination, war, and corruption. It's enough to make you want to throw your hands up in the air and agree with The Bitch when she says, "What can one woman do? Just reach for your blinders or just get depressed about the state of affairs."

I was feeling that way a number of years ago. It was a dreary winter. I was struggling with some family problems and worrying about some troubled patients. I needed a vacation! So I put on my blinders and headed off to sunny Argentina.

During the long flight to Buenos Aires, I read about the natural beauty of the country, the tango, and the cosmopolitan mix of people. But I also read about the chilling recent history of Argentina: In the 1970s a group of generals, known as the junta, overthrew the government and began a reign of terror. Anyone who even questioned the junta was kidnapped, tortured, and killed.

Students handing out protest literature, journalists who criticized junta tactics, lawyers who tried to free prisoners, and even innocent bystanders to protests were in mortal danger. Plainclothes police would come to their houses at night and drag them away. Most victims were never heard from again, so they became known as "the disappeared." The only group brave and effective enough to consistently protest against the junta was the mothers of the disappeared.

I became so fascinated by this example of maternal strength and power that I wound up interviewing some of these women, the Mothers of the Plaza de Mayo. I wanted to understand how a group of relatively uneducated mothers could do what all the more conventionally powerful groups could not: inspire the rest of the country to protest and get rid of oppression. How did they stand up to the voice in their head—I can't call self-preservation a Bitch—that said "be quiet and stay home"? Here's what they told me:

They met by chance as they frantically went from police stations to hospitals to government offices, begging for any information about their sons and daughters who "disappeared." Finally they went to the cardinal at the main cathedral, but he refused to help them.

One Mother said, "It was then that we realized we were on our own. We were the only ones who would try to save our children, so fourteen of us went to protest in front of the Presidential Palace, asking, 'Where is my child?'"

At first, the secret police ignored them because they were "only a group of mothers." But as their group grew over the weeks, the secret police used a tactic that stopped all previous protests: They asked a few women for their identity papers. That was terrifying because it meant the secret police would come for you.

But instead of quickly dispersing, like other protest groups had, all the mothers waved their identity papers, rushed at the police, and demanded to be taken, too. If the police tried to haul off a few mothers, all the rest surrounded the police cars, screaming and demanding that their friends be released. "The police didn't know what to do with us: noisy, crazy women who would not be intimidated," a Mother recalled.

So the police used fire hoses and dogs against the Mothers. They vandalized their houses and made some of them disappear. But the number of protesters continued to grow.

The Argentine press had been muzzled, but the international press quickly picked up the Mothers' story. This put the government in a bind. The junta was trying to pretend that everything was normal in Argentina, so with the foreign press watching, they couldn't make too many of the Mothers disappear. But with more and more women asking, "Where is my child?" it was clear to the world that something was radically wrong.

I asked the Mothers how they counteracted the fear that kept most of their fellow Argentines quiet. One said, "When your child is taken away, you struggle for him and his life. I could not allow myself to look at my fear, because if you start looking at it, you become too fearful to go on."

And how did they counteract The Bitch of hopelessness and depression? "Once I realized that my son was not coming back soon, I, like all the Mothers, realized I had two choices: I could stay at home and cry, or I could go out and struggle," a Mother told me. "And you know it is quite amazing that none of the Mothers in our association ever felt the need to consult a psychologist. Our psychologist was the struggle."

This woman said the fathers, who went to work each day and had to pretend that everything was normal, were the ones who suffered terribly. "Many became so depressed they couldn't work. Many died of heart attacks, cancer, and other illnesses."

My eyes were opened by my interviews with the Mothers. I went on to interview other ordinary women who did extraordinary things in the United States and around the world: stopping wars and fighting hunger, poverty, discrimination, crime, and disease. I compiled these stories in a book called *Mother Power* and found consistent themes.

Each woman started by getting upset or angry about a problem. When her Bitch told her there was nothing she could do about the problem, she decided at least to try.

When her Bitch said no one would listen because she had no credentials or expertise, she realized that even if she lacked a formal education or related credentials, she had natural credibility if she said, "As a mother, I believe . . ." Or "As a woman, I think . . ."

That's so true. If I said, "As a psychologist, I think the media should stop directing blatantly sexual messages to children," I might have some clout. But isn't it stronger to say, "As a psychologist and a mother, I think the media should stop directing blatantly sexual messages to children"? And if the statement only began, "As a mother, I think the media . . ." that would have a lot of power, too.

Other consistent themes included the following: they gathered friends to their cause for support; they didn't try to do it alone; they got the press involved; and they had to be prepared to be tenacious for the long haul. Change almost never came quickly or easily.

Leymah Gbowee, who won a Nobel Prize for leading a group of women who forced Liberian warlords into peace agreements, recently told an audience that anyone intent on creating a movement for social change "can't be afraid if people call you crazy." She said, "Good work is a bright light, and light always attracts a lot of shadows. If you want to know if you are doing good work, look how much criticism you are attracting."

In fact, if you are being a strong, assertive person, some people might even call you a bitch. And since there's usually no way to reason with someone so bigoted that they would confuse strength with bitchiness, the best reply might be one that I read on a T-shirt: "That's Ms. Bitch to you!"

BANISHING THE BITCH

Yes, the world is a troubled place. Yes, you may live in a toxic family or society. But no, you do not have to believe The Bitch when she says you are too weak, stupid, or helpless to change things.

Get support. When The Bitch is in someone else's head, you might need a family member, friend, clergy person, or therapist to validate that you're not crazy or to blame. Other times the best help comes from a hotline or support group. The point is to recognize and get the assistance you need to deal with a toxic friend, parent, classmate, marriage, or society.

You may never get The Bitch completely out of your head, but you can learn how to tame her and tone her down. Then consider reaching out to others, helping to contain the toxicity in their lives or in society. You can start in a very small way—simply joining a group that is working to change things, just being one small cog in the engine of change. You may never want to do more, but at least you are doing something to keep The Bitch under control.

Make the craziness stop with you. I've found that patients who grew up in abusive homes are often afraid that they will be abusive if they have children. In fact, this fear keeps many from becoming parents. But some of the most loving parents I have ever known, including my own, grew up with abuse. They vowed that the abuse that had flowed through previous generations would stop with them. And it did.

So don't let The Bitch make you doubt yourself or keep you from becoming a parent if that's what you want to do. If you find yourself tempted to act the way your parents did, go to an anger management class or therapy.

Never let The Bitch say, "What can one woman do?" or "Why bother?" Counter that defeatism with, "At least I'm going to try!" If we all do a little bit, just think how much can *change*! If you don't believe that one woman can make a difference, here's another story from *Mother Power* that proves you and your Bitch wrong.

One Thanksgiving, a woman named Iris was feeling very grateful that, for the first time in many years, no one was going to get drunk and beat her up. She had recently found the courage to leave an abusive husband and was struggling to support her teenage daughter and grandson in a very poor section of New York. But in the spirit of the holiday, she bought an extra turkey and loaf of bread and handed out sandwiches to the homeless people and prostitutes in her neighborhood.

She said they looked at her with such gratitude that she decided to do this every week. So every Saturday, Iris made a big pot of soup and handed it out to hungry people. But she couldn't afford to keep doing this on her clerk's salary, so she asked a few people to help her.

Soon, people were giving her canned goods and clothes to distribute, and these supplies were crowding her tiny apartment, so she asked her pastor if she could use a closet at the church to store supplies during the week. And as more people began wanting to help her make soup, she asked the pastor if she could cook in the church kitchen.

Well, like the story of the loaves and fishes, Iris's small program grew into a food bank and soup kitchen that feeds hundreds of people every week. When Iris retired, she went back to school to obtain her bachelor's degree. She told me, "I never thought I was smart enough, especially with all the abuse." But now she likes to tell everyone, "If I can do it, you can, too."

Yes, if Iris can do it, you can, too.

15

OLD BITCH

Spoiling the Golden Years

When I told the author and journalist Lynn Sherr the title of this book, she shared a favorite joke: Toward the end of a church service, the minister asked the congregation, "How many of you have forgiven your enemies?" All held up their hands except one small elderly lady.

"Mrs. Jones? Are you not willing to forgive your enemies?"

"I don't have any," she replied, smiling sweetly.

"Mrs. Jones, that is very unusual. How old are you?"

"Ninety-eight," she replied.

"Mrs. Jones, please come down in front and tell us how a person can live ninety-eight years and not have an enemy in the world."

The little sweetheart tottered down the aisle, faced the congregation, and said: "I outlived the bitches."

Hmmm. I spent a bit of time wondering whether the old lady was really "sweet" and had outlived the people who tried to put a Bitch in her head, or whether she was the kind who put a Bitch in others. Regardless, even if you've outlived the bitches in your life, you will undoubtedly have to fight some new Bitches in your head as you age.

Sooner or later after forty, The Bitch will tell you, "You're old and over the hill." Or you will look in the mirror and The Bitch will torture you about the roll that has formed around your middle, or the droopy skin underneath your upper arms, or tell you that the wrinkles around your knees make you look like a camel.

If you are single, she will say things like, "Who would want a wrinkly old bat like you?" Or, "Men always want younger women, so only guys in their nineties would be interested in you." And let's not forget this Bitch favorite: When you forget where you put your keys or the plot of the book you read last week, she says, "You've got Alzheimer's!"

To counter this depressing load of crap, this chapter will present role models who are living life with zest and joy, and the Bitch-proof ideas that propelled them into happy old age.

BITCH-PROOF IDEA #1: PLEASE YOURSELF

Kira was a professor at a college in Chicago. She had a comfortable life with a house, husband, good job, two kids, and a dog. Then, when she was sixty, well before she wanted to retire, the college swept out all the older, better-paid staff like her.

Kira had been in counseling for years, trying to hold together a marriage she described as a "constant struggle and compromise." She said that she stayed in the marriage "because I was distracted by my kids and career." But, she said, she also stayed because "my mother stayed in her marriage with my father who was an alcoholic. That made me feel I shouldn't 'give up the fight.' Plus, I didn't feel strong enough to thrive on my own."

Soon after Kira lost her job, her mother died. "That made me realize life is short. I looked at my husband and realized I didn't want to spend the rest of my life with him. The final straw was when I was hospitalized for appendicitis and he was totally unhelpful. When I got well, I moved out of the house."

Kira's two kids were off on their own, but at least she had her dog to keep her company. Then shortly after she found her own apartment, her dog had to be put down. "Suddenly I had nothing to tie me down. And nobody to blame but myself. So I began to think about how to please myself.

"I had to look at who I really was. And while I have many interests, I realized that, basically, I am a teacher. I am an extrovert who loves to be around people, especially if I am teaching." Kira also realized she was a woman who was starved for adventure. So she joined the Peace Corps.

"The Peace Corps tries to have 10 percent of their volunteers be people over fifty-five with specific skills like teaching," Kira told me. "They sent me to Botswana for two years. In that part of the world, one in four people have AIDS, so I was assigned to a high school to teach a program called Life Skills, helping young people learn how to handle risky situations, sexual and otherwise.

"After two years in Africa, I didn't really fit well when I went back to Chicago. People had gone on with their lives without me. Some friends had died. After a while, I was longing for another adventure, to explore a place where I might fit better."

So Kira found a tenant for her apartment in Chicago and used the rent money to move to New York City for two years. "Again, I had to decide what I wanted, who I was, and what would please me. I decided that while I still love to teach, the arts nourish me. In Brooklyn and Manhattan there is something going on in the arts all the time. And my son lived nearby."

But a few months after Kira moved to Brooklyn, her son received a great job offer in Europe and moved abroad. No problem. By then, Kira had learned self-reliance. She knew she could make it on her own.

"I think the key to a happy retirement is finding a balance of work, learning, and play that pleases you," Kira told me. "I teach as a volunteer in an after-school tutoring program for disadvantaged elementary school kids. I take a painting course where I am learning to use acrylics, and I take a course where I am learning about Asian art. I also love to read and joined a book club through my local library."

Kira is on a relatively limited retirement income, so she looks for courses with special rates for seniors or discounted tickets for events. And the shows at art galleries are always free.

"Almost every day or night I do something stimulating and emotionally nourishing," she says. "Sometimes it is just watching *Frontline* on PBS, but other times it is going to the theater or a museum or gallery. Dance really nourishes me. I go to see a lot of dance performances and I just took a dance improvisation course in Harlem."

Kira's active balance of work and play strikes me as the best way to defeat The Bitch of boredom that haunts so many retirement communities.

BITCH-PROOF IDEA #2:
MAKE POSITIVE PLANS FOR YOUR FUTURE

When English actress Maggie Smith was in her early seventies, she got cancer. Chemo and radiation made her feel so wiped out, she decided to quit acting. When a friend asked, "What about your future?" Smith replied, "Most of my future is behind me." That's the depressing thing The Old Bitch tells many retirees.

Dustin Hoffman went looking for Smith to play a role in his wonderful movie, *Quartet*. Luckily, he convinced her to face down her Old Bitch and come out of retirement, where she not only recovered her sense of future and joy but also snagged many more roles and kudos for parts like her award-winning Duchess in *Downton Abbey*.

For many, like Maggie Smith and Kira, the professor from Chicago, sometimes a joyful future involves finding new ways to use old skills. But often a new life opens up in retirement by doing something completely different. In fact, psychoanalyst Carl Jung suggested that people who have been hard-driving business types should give their life new balance by focusing on what he called "the feminine" things like the arts, mentoring, or helping—either helping to raise children, or helping those in need. On the other hand, people who have been doing "feminine" things should switch to what he called "masculine" endeavors like helping to run an organization or starting a business.

One of the happiest couples I know made one of those "Jungian switches" in retirement. He was a high-powered international lawyer. He started the Russian office for his law firm and lived in a fabulous apartment a block from Red Square. But his law firm had a mandatory retirement age, so he had to leave when he felt he was at the top of his game.

Forced retirement gave The Bitch an opportunity to tell him, "You're over the hill," and "You will just sit around waiting to die." Meanwhile, his wife, who had stayed home to raise their three children, earned the credentials to teach English as a second language just before they moved abroad. So, once again, she put her career on hold for his. But when they returned to the United States, she found a job teaching ESL. In a role reversal that happens to many older couples, suddenly, he was rattling around their home while she was off to work, doing so well that she was eventually made the director of the ESL department.

For a while, The Bitch tormented him, by pointing out that his younger colleagues were still going to work while he had nothing to do until, like Kira, he found a productive way to live the rest of his life.

He decided to continue practicing law, but in a completely different way. He took a few courses on poverty law and offered to work pro bono for a settlement house—a place that serves the poor. He goes there several days a week and works on immigration, domestic abuse, and eviction cases. His new clients pay him nothing but gratitude. But that has made for a rich life.

Other people, like songwriter Carole King, find that in their older years they are happy to leave their professions behind. When King came to see the Broadway smash, *Beautiful*, based on her life, she told the *New York Times* that she no longer writes. "I don't feel there's a calling for me to do that now," she said. "I feel like I've said everything I need to say." But she hasn't done everything she needs to do. She lives in Idaho and is very active in projects that try to protect the environment.

Similarly, a teacher named Margaret, who had always taught little kids, was surprised when she realized she no longer wanted to do that. "When I retired and moved to Florida," she told me, "I began volunteering at a play school. I felt guilty when I wanted to stop after a year. The school had paid for me to get certified in Florida and I felt I had wasted their money.

"I used to love playing with small children; in fact, it felt like I *needed* to do it. But after a year of volunteering, I realized that was over. I wanted to do something else."

For the first time in many years, Margaret is able to be a student, not a teacher. She takes courses at a Senior Citizens' center in line dancing, knitting, computers, and Russian history. She joined a choral group and belly dancing class, often going with those groups to perform in nursing homes.

The key to a happy retirement, no matter whether you are famous like Maggie Smith and Carole King or "just" an ordinary teacher or lawyer, is to look for new challenges and look forward to new experiences. That's what makes people feel like they have a promising future. So if The Old Bitch is telling you that you are over the hill, confound her by planning a future with new hills to climb.

BITCH-PROOF IDEA #3:
DON'T BE AFRAID TO TRY AND FAIL

When Dana Dakin, the founder of a micro-loan program called Women's Trust, was in her late forties, she met the head of the Ford Foundation Endowments program. "He was about to retire and he said, 'I believe that life is in thirds. The first third, you learn. The second third, you earn. And the last third, you return.' That shot me through the heart," Dana told me. "I decided when I hit my third stage, that was what I wanted to do."

Dana tucked away that idea for years as she worked as a marketing consultant with investment funds. In her late fifties, she was happily living in a restored firehouse in a small town in New Hampshire. But in 2002, when she turned fifty-nine, she felt something was missing in her life.

"I was starting to feel what many older women feel—invisible, discarded. Those negative thoughts you call The Bitch. I call them my 'second guesser.' I had to tell my second guesser, 'Wait a minute! There's a lot I've got to do. I just don't know what it is.'"

Dana wasn't rich, but she felt it was time to begin giving back to the world in some way. And she decided that by the time she turned sixty, she would have figured it out.

"I had the example of a woman I knew who had gone to Nepal when she was sixty. She saw the poverty there: women who were street cleaners and began work at four or five in the morning with their children alongside and babies strapped to their backs. She decided to start a day care center for those women. Now she's eighty-seven and still going strong. I used her as an inspiration. But it wasn't exactly clear to me what I wanted to do."

Dana read about micro-lending programs that give very small loans so very poor women can strengthen their small businesses in developing countries. As a businesswoman, that idea appealed to her. She told me, "I was a successful woman entrepreneur and decided to help other women be the same.

"I thought about how I had been on a safari in Africa once and seen the grinding poverty there. And one morning I woke up with the whole idea: you are going to Africa; find a village and start a micro-loan program!" But Dana knew people would think she was crazy to think about doing something like this.

Still, she persisted by setting criteria for the country she would like to explore. It had to be English speaking so she could communicate and it had to be relatively safe and stable with a reasonable legal system. Plus it had to have an economy where a small amount of money could make a big difference in a person's life.

She said, "There are fifty-three countries in Africa, and in the end, Ghana was the one that met my criteria." But she didn't know anyone there. So she began networking and talking to anyone she could meet who had any connection to Ghana: a professor, a nun, and her former fitness trainer whose father lived in Ghana.

As Dana's sixtieth birthday approached, she had not been able to talk to anyone who actually lived in Ghana, but she decided if she didn't act on her dream, it might slip away. "So I booked a flight and was in Ghana two months after my sixtieth birthday. Upon arrival, I reached my trainer's father on the phone, and he said, 'We have been waiting for you.'"

He had gone to a village where he knew the chief, talked to the elders, and found a place for her to stay. So she checked out of her hotel and he drove her there. That's how she chose Pokuase, a place where 20,000 people live twenty miles from Accra, the capital of Ghana.

After staying in Pokuase, Dana returned home to New Hampshire, established a non-profit organization, and sold her second car for $18,000 to finance the loan program. "The second guesser told me, 'You're going to look stupid by throwing all that money away on such a long shot.' But I had a retirement fund to fall back on and the money I got for the car was money I didn't *have* to have."

Dana started by hiring a local woman in Pokuase to help her find her first loan recipients. The recipients formed foursomes to support each other in their business efforts—and also to make sure that the loans were repaid so they could apply for a second, larger loan.

Dana started small. The initial seventy-two women recipients received a total of $1,500 in loans. Many of those loans were only $20 or $30, enough to buy produce for resale at the local market, or a bolt of cloth to make into dresses. The women were expected to repay their loan in four months with 13–15 percent interest. The program was successful from the start with a repayment rate over 80 percent.

Dana triumphed over her second guesser. In the first five years of operation, over one thousand women in Pokuase received small business loans, two hundred and fifty women and girls were given educational scholarships or enrolled in skill-building workshops, and eight hundred women and girls gained access to improved health care through a clinic Women's Trust set up in the village.

When people in Dana's town in New Hampshire heard about what she was doing, instead of saying she was crazy, they offered to help. Retired executives traveled to Ghana to teach courses in small business management. Dentists, nurses, and physicians used their vacations to staff the clinic. And MBA professors came to learn how to start similar programs in other small towns.

Ten years after starting Women's Trust, Dana stepped down and turned it over to a board of directors to run. She is now doing pro-bono consulting with other projects in Africa, helping a group in Angola build a church and community center and a group in Liberia strengthen a micro-lending program.

For fun, Dana has begun taking cross-country road trips with a friend of hers who is equally interested in micro-credit. As they travel around, laugh, and meet individuals contributing to their local communities, she is writing a workbook that will help other people replicate her program in Ghana. I hope that book will include a section on quieting "the second guesser," or as we know her, "The Bitch," so other people won't think their ideas would be a crazy waste of time and money.

BITCH-PROOF IDEA #4:
SHARE YOUR TALENTS, TIME, AND KNOWLEDGE

Lynda Doery graduated from Smith and headed to Manhattan, dreaming of becoming a dancer on Broadway. After snagging a few minor roles and teaching children's dance classes, she married a man whose career took them all over the country. As soon as she settled into each new house, she would begin to take dance classes and teach them, too. This pattern continued when she and her husband retired to Sarasota, Florida. But when her husband was diagnosed with an aggressive cancer, Lynda stopped teaching and devoted herself to nursing him.

After he died, Lynda settled into a relatively solitary life. "Even though I was a performer, I am really quite shy . . . an introvert," Lynda told me. "So while I missed my husband terribly, I was comfortable being home alone, reading and gardening. Then a neighbor asked me to join the Fine Arts Society. After that, I was asked to get involved with Girls, Inc., a charity that helps disadvantaged children. I wanted to say no and just live my quiet life, but I realized that would be selfish. This was not about me; it was about kids who needed help."

As a psychologist, I have found that all too often when men and women stop working, they become very fearful about working again. Their Bitch tells them things like, "You can't cut it anymore" or "They will find out you're over the hill." Lynda's Bitch told her, "Getting involved would be too tiring for you," but she was determined to act in the face of her fear. "I knew that as a widow, it would be good for me to get out in the community. So I started a dance class for the girls, and as people asked me to do more, I forced myself to say yes. It's paid off."

In the thirteen years since her husband died, Lynda has joined the boards of several civic and arts organizations. When I walked around town with her and her second husband, people knew her everywhere we went and said hello. She is clearly a beloved member of her community.

Lynda says she's still an introvert, although her friends would probably never guess. "So even though I'm no longer a practicing Jew, I keep the Sabbath by staying quiet on Saturdays and Sundays. I take care of my plants, study French, research dance on the Internet, and read. Of course, sometimes something like a wonderful party will keep me from doing these quiet things I love to do."

Remember the old adage, "all work and no play makes Jack a dull boy"? Well, unfortunately when people are retired, I have found that all play and no work make Jack and Jill depressed. So, Lynda was smart to force herself to engage in volunteer work outside the home—and balance it with the alone time that nourishes her.

BITCH-PROOF IDEA #5: WRITE A HAPPY ENDING TO YOUR LIFE STORY

The stories I have told so far are about people who still have their health. If you have become infirm, it's much more difficult to battle The Bitch and live life fully to the end. But one way to do this is to create your legacy.

I'm not talking about how much money you will leave to children and charities; I'm talking about how your family and friends will remember you. We all have the opportunity to be a shining example of living positively to the end.

One of the kindest things you can do for your family is to get your paperwork in order. If your Bitch is saying, "It's too overwhelming! You can't face this!" hire someone to help you sort through things. If you can't afford to hire help, do it yourself in small steps: just a half hour a day. Schedule that half hour early in the morning when you are not tired or bogged down. Don't let anything interfere with your half-hour clean up. And then give yourself a treat as a reward for the half-hour job well done.

Don't be surprised if once you get into the task of setting things straight, you don't want to stop after a half hour. But if you can only do a half hour a day, that's fine. That is much, much better than doing nothing.

Be sure to put all your financial records, your will, and your health care proxies in one place. Any hospital can give you an "Advance Medical Directive" (living will) and a "Durable Power of Attorney for Health Care," which designates the person you want to carry out your medical wishes. These forms tell your loved ones what kind of end-of-life care you want. They will be so grateful that you have spared them the guilt of not taking extraordinary measures if you don't want them.

None of the above is fun, but it's something that your children will respect you for doing. So now here's a fun thing your children will also be grateful for: write your family history and personal memoir.

You are linked to a long line of relatives, winding back through history into the earliest times. You may not know anything other than your grandparents' names or you may have a whole genealogical tree. Whatever you have, it's time to write down everything you know about the people who came before you. Names, places of origin, professions, dates, plus any colorful stories you have heard. You can even illustrate this with old pictures.

If your Bitch is saying, "Why bother?" or "It's too much work," or "Who would be interested in any of this old stuff?" just think: Aren't you sorry that your parents and grandparents didn't do this for you?

It's also time to write your personal story. Everyone's life is like a novel with main characters, scoundrels, heroes, funny anecdotes, and pivotal events. Include a happy ending—love notes to all the people you will leave behind when you die. Your memories, and your memory, will be treasured forever.

BANISHING THE BITCH

Every age and stage has its challenges and rewards, but the most difficult one comes last. There are so many losses: friends die, bodies droop and ache, and it's frightening to come to terms with death. Many people just drown their fears with too much alcohol or round-the-clock TV. Others spend their lives going from one doctor to another, as The Bitch makes them fear every ache and pain.

And then there are the people we all admire: the ones who stay vital, whether they are healthy or not. Everyone *wants* to be around them. You have learned some of their Bitch-defeating methods in this chapter, but here are some more:

Find role models. When I was in my twenties, I began to be fascinated by people who didn't lose their zest and joy as they aged. Call me a long-term planner, but even then I wanted to learn how they did it, so I could try to be like them.

One of my supervisors in graduate school was an eminent eighty-year-old psychiatrist who retained his vigor by being as interested in what his students had to say as in teaching us all that he had learned.

Another role model was my cousin, Fran, who was my parents' age. She loved giving dinner parties that mixed people in their twenties like me with older people from business and the arts. When she had to move into a retirement home, she retained her active involvement in politics, the theater, and with friends by riding the bus two hours each way into Manhattan every week.

Once, when we met for lunch, I told her how much I admired her and asked how she kept her youthful spirit and enthusiasm. "I try to make it look easy and not complain," she said after a pause, "but because I love you I'll tell you the truth: it's really hard. The older I get, the more I just want to stay in bed in the morning. I have to force myself to take the bus to see old friends or go to a museum. But I'm not going to give in."

I appreciated her candor. Now I know that if I get into my eighties, and my Old Bitch tries to say, "Oh, don't bother, you're too tired," I will counter with, "If Fran can stay cool through her eighties, why shouldn't I?"

Quit playing "Ain't it awful?" Here's the bad news: No one wants to hear you complain about your bunions. If your Bitch has made you think your medical woes are fascinating conversation, put a Band-Aid over your mouth.

No complaining about where you live, either. A woman in a beach section of Florida where signs proclaim that it's "paradise" said she has a friend who complains all the time. The restaurants are always too noisy. She thinks it's terrible how kids chase sea gulls on the beach. "I really have started to avoid her," the woman told me. "It just isn't pleasant."

While some older people enjoy playing the game of "Ain't it awful," competing to see who feels worse, or whose children are the most ungrateful, if you are beginning to want to play this game, get a medication consultation for an antidepressant. Negative thinking, complaining, and unhappiness are frequently unrecognized symptoms of depression.

Invest your time wisely. No matter how much money you have, your most precious asset is time. It's running out. Your Bitch can make you terrified of that fact. But don't forget what you've learned in other chapters: the people who are most afraid of dying are the people who don't feel like they are really living.

So, ask yourself some important questions: What do you want to do with the rest of your life? What experiences do you want to have before you die? Is there anything you want to say to anyone?

Give each of these questions serious thought. Better yet, sit down with a pen and paper and make some notes. Then make plans so that when the time comes, you will be able to die as peacefully and with as few regrets as possible. That's a Bitch-proof goal.

16

DING DONG, THE BITCH IS DEAD

(And How to Keep Her That Way)

By now, I hope you have identified your Bitch, the discouraging, critical voice in your head, and the ways she harms your life. I also hope you are well on the way to replacing The Bitch with an encouraging inner voice that sounds like a good parent, friend, and coach. This new voice should allow you to enjoy and appreciate who you are while you are working to improve.

Now you're ready for the life-long maintenance program to keep The Bitch from sneaking back into your head. So this chapter will tell you the important elements that keep The Bitch at bay.

IDENTIFY CONSTRUCTIVE VERSUS DESTRUCTIVE CRITICISM

Everyone makes mistakes. Everyone has problems and areas they want to improve. Constructive criticism identifies what needs to be changed without being insulting and sets positive goals that are reasonable to achieve. Destructive criticism is what The Bitch specializes in: making you feel so bad that it's hard to summon the energy and creativity to change. The acid test is this: only offer criticism to yourself in the positive terms you would use to motivate your child or your friend.

Listen for insults. Become extremely aware if you're using words like *lazy*, *stupid*, *friendless*, *ugly*, or *fat*—and stop the thought right there! Either switch to an affirmation to counter the insult—or make a plan to correct the problem. If you have made a plan, insist on loving yourself as you are while you execute the plan.

Remember, for example, what you learned in the chapter "Beauty and The Bitch": People who decide they can accept their body as it is put themselves in a no-lose situation. They usually are more successful in sticking to their healthy eating plan than self-critical people who depress themselves and then crave comfort in food. Even if they don't trim down, they are happier than people who hate their bodies.

MAKE UP YOUR OWN
WORD IF YOU DON'T LIKE *BITCH*

People you have read about in previous chapters have used "the undercutter," "the devil on my shoulder," and "the mean girl." Arianna Huffington, speaking about her book *Thrive*, recently told an audience that the negative self-talk in a woman's head is The Obnoxious Roommate who criticizes everything you do, the one who makes you think you need to be perfect and attacks you if you make a mistake. As she said, "You have to tell that obnoxious roommate to finally leave."

I agree. I often tell patients that just as you would never allow a critical, mean, undercutting person to live with you in your home, you should never allow The Bitch—or The Obnoxious Roommate—to live in your head. I hope this book has helped you kick her out, and this chapter will help you padlock the door, so she can't sneak back in.

BITCH-PROOFING YOUR
LIFE IS SERIOUS BUSINESS

Just because I have used a light tone and told some jokes about The Bitch doesn't mean that I don't understand how she can literally be a killer. She not only kills joy, but also, if she causes a deep depression or convinces someone to put up with abuse, people can die. Sometimes it's helpful to lighten life with a joke, but The Bitch is no laughing matter.

IT MAY BE VERY DIFFICULT
TO ROOT OUT YOUR BITCH

Even experts have trouble eliminating The Bitch. A consultant, who gives problem-solving workshops at major corporations, teaches executives to state situations in positive terms, because that helps them find solutions. "I teach, for example, that instead of saying, 'My employees are lazy,' or 'My people can't seem to get to work on time,' you will be more effective if you say, 'How can I get everyone to be at their desks by 8:30?'"

But the consultant told me, "I find myself being negative in my personal life, saying things like, 'I'll never be able to get a reservation' or 'They will never give my deposit back.' When I think about it, I know it's so much better to think, 'I want this, so I have to do that,' rather than discourage myself from even trying."

So don't get discouraged if your Bitchy habits die hard. It takes persistence to teach yourself to be more positive. But you will feel so much better when you succeed!

WHEN YOU RELAPSE,
GET BACK ON THE WAGON

Some therapists claim that a relapse is actually beneficial. When patients start to feel better, they forget how bad they felt when they were depressed or anxious. A relapse reminds them how their life has improved and motivates them to keep going.

It's the same with Bitchy thoughts. A relapse can remind you how mean you were to yourself, how awful it felt, and how important it is to never go back to treating yourself that way again.

PREPARE TO BE A
LIFELONG BITCH DETECTIVE

Once you have identified the most obvious ways your Bitch has been torturing you, you may begin to hear the more subtle ways she undercuts you. Have fun with this, using an "Aha! Gotcha!" approach instead of getting discouraged and thinking you will never be free of her.

Don't be embarrassed to tell Bitch stories about yourself. Almost every woman I talked to had a Bitch story that they felt relieved to share. Have fun discussing this with your friends and catching The Bitch when you hear her discouraging your relatives and buddies.

Can you imagine how great it would be if we lived in a Bitch-free society? How the quality of life, and probably even the economy, would improve if we all felt freer to pursue our dreams? After all, our constitution guarantees the right to life, liberty, and the pursuit of happiness. So leave your Bitch-baggage behind, and go for it!

LET'S HELP EACH OTHER

I realize that this subject is much too big for one book. So if I didn't include your Bitch, please write me and tell me about her. I am planning a sequel and want to include as many new stories as I can. So please visit my website TheBitchInYourHead.com and tell me yours. If you want to remain anonymous, I won't use your name.

I would also like to speak by Skype to as many book groups and organizations as possible. And I particularly like speaking in person at fundraisers for worthy causes. Now that I have my public speaking Bitch out of my head, I find it fun to interact with audiences and I'm told that I'm good at it. So feel free to visit the website and get in touch with me if you are interested in having me speak to your book group or organization.

BOOK GROUP QUESTIONS

1. What do you think of labeling self-criticism, The Bitch? Can you think of a better name?
2. What are the worst ways The Bitch affects women?
3. What are the worst ways The Bitch affects men?
4. Why do you think The Bitch influences women more than men?
5. Did Dr. Plumez fail to mention any important areas affected by The Bitch?
6. Is there any way The Bitch is helpful?
7. How has The Bitch affected your life?
8. What is the best way of ridding oneself of The Bitch?
9. Should we ask Dr. Plumez to spend a few minutes with our book group via Skype?

ACKNOWLEDGMENTS

I want to thank all the people who generously shared their Bitch stories with me. While I met some men who didn't seem to understand the concept, even extremely self-confident and successful women seemed relieved to open up and tell me how they wrestled with their Bitch. Some were happy to let me use their names. Others wanted to remain anonymous, so in those cases I have disguised their names and identifying information. My colleagues at the Westchester County Psychological Association have been particularly supportive and helpful.

I also want to thank my wonderful agent, Janet Rosen at Sheree Bykofsky Associates, and the talented editor, Lara Asher, who first loved The Bitch. Their enthusiasm and expertise was absolutely invaluable.

A number of people at Rowman & Littlefield have been instrumental in bringing The Bitch to life: Rick Rinehart, Karie Simpson, Janice Braunstein, Kalen Landow, and Sharon Kunz.

Last, but certainly not least, I want to thank Adrienne Skinner and Joe Ha, the talented entrepreneurs who created Book Banter, a social media/web site to market books. They chose *The Bitch in Your Head* to launch their company, and I am very grateful.

BIBLIOGRAPHY

CHAPTER 1: INTRODUCING THE BITCH

Freedman, Rita. *Body Love*. Carlsbad, CA: Gurze Books, 2002.

Frieze, I. H., et al. "Assessing the Theoretical Models for Sex Differences in Causal Attributions for Success and Failure." *Sex Roles* 8, no. 4 (1982).

Kay, Katty, and Claire Shipman. *The Confidence Code*. New York: Random House, 2014.

Sandberg, Sheryl. *Lean In*. New York: Knopf, 2013.

CHAPTER 2: LITTLE BITCH

Burns, Ken. "Interview: Meryl Streep." *USA Weekend*, December 1, 2002, 20–21.

Clance, Pauline. *The Imposter Phenomenon*. Atlanta: Peachtree Publishers, 1985. https://counseling.caltech.edu/general/infoandResources//Imposter.

Kilbourne, Jean. *Deadly Persuasion*. New York: Free Press, 1999.

Levin, Diane, and Jean Kilbourne. *So Sexy So Soon*. New York: Random House, 2009.

Pipher, Mary. *Reviving Ophelia*. New York: Putnam, 1994.

Sandberg, Sheryl. *Lean In*. New York: Knopf, 2013.

CHAPTER 3: BEAUTY AND THE BITCH

"Comfortable with Her Curves." *Mail Online*, March 28, 2014, 1–9.

Ephron, Delia. "The Imperfect Paradise." *International Herald Tribune*, September 10, 2013, 7.

Sandanger, I., et al. "Is Women's Mental Health More Susceptible than Men's to the Influence of Surrounding Stress?" *Social Psychiatry Epidemiology* 39 (March 2004): 177–84.

"Stars Prove Nobody's Perfect!" *In Touch*, April 14, 2014, 44–45.

Szubanski, Magda. *The Moth Radio Hour*. National Public Radio, March 23, 2014.

Tomiyama, Janet, Mary Dalliman, and Elissa Epel. "Comfort Food Is Comforting to Those Most Stressed: Evidence of the Chronic Stress Response Network in High-Stress Women." *Psychoneuroendocrinology* 36, no. 10 (2011): 1513–19.

Vega, Tanzina. "Ad about Women's Self-Image Creates a Sensation." *New York Times*, April 19, 2013, B1, B6.

Wong, Adele. "Editor's Note." *Epicure*, September 18, 2013, 10.

CHAPTER 4: BITCH OF A DATE

Carnegie, Dale. *How to Win Friends and Influence People*. New York: Simon & Schuster, 1936.

"Dating Science." *New York Magazine*, February 11, 2013, 54–55.

Garcia, Justin, et al. "Sexual Hook-Up Culture." *Monitor on Psychology* (February 2013): 62–67.

Kitroeff, Natalie. "In Hookups, Inequality Still Reigns." *New York Times*, November 12, 2013, D1, D5.

"The List: 25 Stars Who Have Tried Online Dating." *US Weekly*, March 31, 2014, 20.

Raitt, Bonnie. *The Luck of the Draw*. Capitol, 1991, compact disc.

CHAPTER 5: BITCH AND CHAIN

Cambridge Women's Pornography Collective. *Porn for Women*. San Francisco: Chronicle Books, 2007.

Chapman, Gary. *The 5 Love Languages*. Chicago: Northfield Publishers, 1992.

Rubenstein, Carin. *The Superior Wife Syndrome*. New York: Simon & Schuster, 2009.

CHAPTER 6: THE PARENTING BITCH

Allegheny Department of Human Services. "Diffuse Mistreatment with 'One Kind Word.'" *DHS News*, April 2014. http://www.alleghenycounty.us/DHS AboutDHS.aspx?id=40911.

Chess, Stella, and Alexander Thomas. *Know Your Child.* New York: Basic Books, 1987.

Duclos, Melissa. "Confessions of a Facebook Mom." *Cleaver Magazine,* September 3, 2013, 1–5.

Grant, Adam. "Raising a Moral Child." *International New York Times,* April 12–13, 2014, 9.

Hogg, Tracy. *Secrets of the Baby Whisperer.* New York: Ballantine Books, 2005.

Maynard, Joyce. *At Home in the World.* New York: Macmillan, 2010.

Reiffel, Suzanne, et al. www.Toolkitsforkids.com.

Watson, Rhoda. *Along the Road to Peace: Fifteen Years with the Peace People.* Belfast: Community of Peace People, 1991.

Winerman, Lea. "Primed for Parenting." *Monitor on Psychology* 44, no. 8 (September 2013): 28–31.

CHAPTER 7: THE BITCH AT WORK

"Former Bank Executive: Women, Ask for a Raise!" *Morning Edition.* National Public Radio, April 7, 2014.

Frieze, I. H., et al. "Assessing the Theoretical Models for Sex Differences in Causal Attributions for Success and Failure." *Sex Roles* 8, no. 4 (1982).

Kass, Sharon. "Employees Perceive Women as Better Managers than Men, Finds Five-Year Study." *American Psychological Association Monitor* (September 1999): 6.

Marritz, Ilya. "A Look at Sleep Deprivation, Wall Street Style." *The Takeaway.* National Public Radio, April 2, 2014.

Plumez, Jacqueline Hornor. *Divorcing a Corporation: How to Know When—and if—a Job Change Is Right for You.* New York: Villard Books, 1985.

"The Truth about the Pay Gap." *New York Times,* April 10, 2014, A24.

CHAPTER 8: SPORTY BITCH

Crouse, Karen. "Swimmer Retires Again, Seeking Normalcy." *Times Digest,* January 26, 2013, 10.

Fisher-Baum, Reuben. "Infographic: Is Your State's Highest-Paid Employee a Coach (Probably)?" http://deadspin.com/infographic-is-your-states-highest-paid-employee-a-co489635228.

Garner, Dwight. "The Legend on the N.B.A. Logo, Running Scared." *New York Times,* November 2, 2011, C3.

Longman, Jeré. "An Involuntary Union of Football Rivals for Philadelphia High Schools." *New York Times*, August 4, 2013. http://www.nytimes.com/2013/08/04/sports/an-involuntary-union-of-rivals-for-philadelphia-high-schools.html?pagewanted=all8_r=0.

Perez-Pena, Richard. "In a Buyer's Market, Colleges Become Fluent in the Language of Business." *New York Times*, March 28, 2014, A12.

Plumez, Jacqueline Hornor. *Mother Power*. Naperville, IL: Sourcebooks, 2002.

"Quotes: Second Place Is for Losers." http://tvtropes.org/pmwiki/pmwiki.php/Quotes/SecondPlaceIsForLosers.

Schwartz, Nelson, and Steve Eder. "College Athletes Aim to Put Price on 'Priceless.'" *New York Times*, April 23, 2014, A1.

We Could Be King. Directed by Judd Ehrlich. Flatbush Pictures, 2014.

West, Jerry, and Jonathan Coleman. *West by West: My Charmed, Tormented Life*. Boston: Little, Brown, 2011.

Wikipedia. "Grantland Rice." http://en.wikipedia.org/wiki/Grantland_Rice.

CHAPTER 9: THE BLAME BITCH

Dominus, Susan. "Portraits of Reconciliation." *New York Time Magazine*, April 4, 2014. http://www.nytimes.com/interactive/2014/04/06/magazine.

Plumez, Jacqueline Hornor. *Divorcing a Corporation: How to Know When—and if—a Job Change Is Right for You*. New York: Villard Books, 1985.

"Restitution." http://www.aardvarc.org/victim/restitution.shtml.

CHAPTER 10: THE BITCH AT NIGHT

BrainyQuote. "John Steinbeck Quotes." http://www.brainyquote.com/quotes/authors/j/john_steinbeck.htm.

Leary, Ann. *The Good House*. New York: St. Martin's, 2013.

CHAPTER 11: THE PARTY BITCH

Metcalfe, Gayden. *Being Dead Is No Excuse*. New York: Miramax, 2005.

Wadler, Joyce. "It's August, They're Coming for You." *New York Times*, August 12, 2009. www.nytimes.com/2009/O8/13guess.html?.

CHAPTER 12: BITCH-A-PHOBIA

Allen, Woody. "Hypochondria: An Inside Look." *New York Times*, January 13, 2013, SR8.
Neuman, Fredric. *Worried Sick?* Hollywood, FL: Simon & Brown, 2008.

CHAPTER 13: SICK BITCH

Carr, Kris. *Crazy Sexy Cancer Tips.* Guilford, CT: Skirt!, 2007.

CHAPTER 14: THE BITCH IN SOMEONE ELSE'S HEAD

Brockes, Emma. "And Now, Wendy Gets Her Chronicles." *New York Times*, August 18, 2011, C1, C4.
Plumez, Jacqueline Hornor. *Mother Power.* Naperville, IL: Sourcebooks, 2002.

CHAPTER 15: OLD BITCH

Jung, Carl. "The Stages of Life." In *Collected Works*. Vol. 8, *Structure and Dynamics of the Psyche*. Edited and translated by Gerhard Adler and R. F. C. Hull. Princeton, NJ: Princeton University Press, 1960.
Pogrebin, Robin. "So Far Away: No, She's in Row K." *New York Times*, April 5, 2014, C1, C6.
"*Quartet*: Dustin Hoffman, behind the Camera." *Fresh Air*. National Public Radio, January 15, 2013.
Story Preservation Initiative. http://storypreservation.wordpress.com/2011/12/27/dana-dakin-?-founder-and-president-?-womenstrust/

CHAPTER 16: DING DONG, THE BITCH IS DEAD

Huffington, Arianna. *Thrive.* New York: Random House, 2014.

ABOUT THE AUTHOR

Fred Doery

Dr. Jacqueline Hornor Plumez is an award-winning psychologist. Her five hundred colleagues in the Westchester County Psychological Association have named her their Distinguished Psychologist and also given her their Distinguished Service award. She has a Ph.D. in psychology from Columbia University and an undergraduate degree in Business Administration from Bucknell. She has been a non-fiction writer almost as long as she's been a practicing psychologist. Her three previous books are *Successful Adoption*, *Divorcing a Corporation*, and *Mother Power*. She has written advice columns for magazines and also for online and traditional newspapers including Gannett's eleven flagship papers, and her articles have appeared in places like *Ladies' Home Journal* and *The New York Times Magazine*.